Updated and Expanded Edition

W9-DBJ-103

+1

Google+ for Business

Second Edition

How Google's
Social Network
Changes Everything

Chris Brogan

QUE®

800 East 96th Street
Indianapolis, Indiana 46240 USA

Google+ for Business, Second Edition

Copyright © 2013 by Chris Brogan

ISBN-13: 978-0-7897-5006-8
ISBN-10: 0-7897-5006-6

The Library of Congress Cataloging-in-Publication data is on file.

Printed in the United States of America

First Printing: October 2012

Trademarks

Warning and Disclaimer

Bulk Sales

Que Publishing offers excellent discounts on this book when ordered in quantity for bulk purchases or special sales. For more information, please contact

> U.S. Corporate and Government Sales
> 1-800-382-3419
> corpsales@pearsontechgroup.com

For sales outside of the U.S., please contact

> International Sales
> international@pearsoned.com

CONTENTS AT A GLANCE

TABLE OF CONTENTS

About the Author

Chris Brogan is a *New York Times* bestselling author and professional speaker, as well as president of Human Business Works. He has been involved with social networks since the bulletin board services of the 1980s and started blogging in 1998, when it was called journaling. Chris cofounded the international unconference experience, PodCamp, which teaches media making and its value to people all over the world. He keynotes at many major corporate events, as well as several technology and web culture events.

Dedication

To everyone who brings a positive view of the world to their surroundings. And to Jacqueline, for believing.

Acknowledgments

Thanks to Katherine Bull, for suggesting I could do this, and to Ginny Munroe, for helping me make it all work better.

We Want to Hear from You!

As the reader of this book, *you* are our most important critic and commentator. We value your opinion and want to know what we're doing right, what we could do better, what areas you'd like to see us publish in, and any other words of wisdom you're willing to pass our way.

As an editor-in-chief for Que Publishing, I welcome your comments. You can email or write me directly to let me know what you did or didn't like about this book—as well as what we can do to make our books better.

Please note that I cannot help you with technical problems related to the topic of this book. We do have a User Services group, however, where I will forward specific technical questions related to the book.

When you write, please be sure to include this book's title and author as well as your name, email address, and phone number. I will carefully review your comments and share them with the author and editors who worked on the book.

Email: feedback@quepublishing.com

Mail: Que Publishing
            ATTN: Reader Feedback
            800 East 96th Street
            Indianapolis, IN 46240 USA

Reader Services

Visit our website and register this book at quepublishing.com/register for convenient access to any updates, downloads, or errata that might be available for this book.

Introduction

How do I convince you to get interested in Google+? How do I convince you that this is important to consider, even if you ultimately choose not to use the service? How can I tell you what I might have missed or underestimated from the first edition of this book? I'm writing this at 33,000 feet, which is where I do a lot of my writing. I took a few deep breaths, and thought, "What should I say to entice people to buy this book about using Google+?" And with that, I discovered a problem.

You see, for the first time in my experiences with social networks and social media (which is over a decade and counting), I'm running into people everywhere who are saying, "I'm just not interested in joining another social network." I hear this from executives at huge companies, from my fellow "play with every new toy" social media types, and from the mom-and-pop stores. In most cases, people use a belligerent voice (I'll admit that it is a whining voice), and they almost always add, "I just figured out Facebook."

Right or wrong, I tend to answer in a somewhat smart-alecky way: "So, how's that AOL working out for you? Can I be one of your top eight on MySpace?" My point is that companies don't get to vote on which social networks people will adopt. They simply have to equip themselves to adapt to new channels as they appear.

Wow, way to sell that book to them, Brogan.

Here's the real story, and I'll tell you this the way I tell this to people in closed rooms for lots and lots of money: If you don't jump into Google+ and start figuring it out now, you'll be behind by the time everyone else shows up. If you doubt for a moment that the world's largest search engine (Google), where 68 percent of all business start looking for *you*, is going to give up easily on the whole "build a useful social network" project, think again. Google has tied the success of Google+ to the annual reviews of several senior staffers, and understanding how people share information on social networks is a huge component to how Google has changed how they do search.

Although I don't compare Google+ to Facebook much (they're both social networks, that's about it), I will say that even though Facebook nears a billion users, Google+ has a huge embedded user base with Android mobile devices (both smartphones and tablets) and they've baked Google+ into several of their flagship Google offerings such as Gmail, YouTube, and more. If you don't see these secret indicators as Google meaning business with Google+, and if you're a business that seeks to do more via the digital channel or you just want to be found via search results, then I'm not sure I can convince you.

I'll tell you some other ditties that might convince you, though:

- The top experts on search engine optimization actively use Google+ and are figuring out its mysteries.
- More small businesses are creating personal pages and business pages to build relationships with potential buyers.
- The President of the U.S., Archbishop Desmond Tutu, and many more notable people have taken to showing up on live Google+ Hangouts on air to share their thoughts.
- Celebrities and entertainment professionals have shown up.
- My own personal "regular people" index (I measure how many non-techies use the service) is going up.

If you're even vaguely curious about using Google+, it's time to get in and start setting up shop. There's money to be made. There's gold in these hills. Come on, let's get some.

—**Chris Brogan** (somewhere between Boston and Chicago in seat 21A)

How Did I Get Here?

You should be a bit skeptical about starting with yet another social network. And it's not like I know every person picking up this book, but some of you just started figuring out Facebook not too long ago and maybe still don't understand what all the fuss is about Twitter. And here comes another living-in-his-own-world marketer/business guy telling you that Google+ is where it's at, right?

I've decided to make the first chapter of this book a bit of an answer to the question "why?" because I think it's important. Whenever you hear the buzz about something new, that's probably the first big question that rushes into your head. Why should I have to know about this? Why must I spend even more time typing into yet another box? What can all this mean for my business?

Another reason I wanted to start this book with some answers to your potential skepticism is because I've felt that, too. I started blogging in 1998, when it was called journaling, which might be reasonably early for blogging, but isn't that early for someone having a web presence, meaning, I wasn't much of an early adopter.

In 2006, I was reasonably early (but not bleeding-edge early) to Twitter, which I came to believe, with all my heart, was going to change business communications and marketing. Because I started so early, I was right about that. It made a great difference to my business, and I helped lots of other companies (and some individuals) figure out how Twitter could add business value.

But for the last few years, I've been asked at every keynote presentation and corporate meeting I've spoken at: What's the next big thing? I haven't been able to answer that question. In every single case, I've answered in a kind of mumble that "I don't actually know what's next, but I'm quite convinced that mobile platforms are big, and uh, I would never bet that either Twitter or Facebook would be forever." I haven't had a good answer to "What's the next big thing?" until now.

I'm just as surprised as you.

Why Is Google+ the Next Big Thing?

I'm not a Google insider, by the way, so this all comes from a passionate user's seat outside the Googleplex. I know nothing more than most users. I have no secret in. What I *do* have, in abundance, is the ability to extrapolate and speculate, and that's part of what fuels my answer.

First, the easy stuff. Google+ is a social network indexed by Google. In recent years, Google searched for ways to amplify the way humans pass links and data inside social networks, which is different than how one page references another page for a search. Stated more simply: Google+ is tied to Google search, so by using it well you can improve your primary website's findability for folks searching for it.

Second, what's probably the least obvious but most powerful part of Google+ is how much of it is built toward making it easy for people to discover you and connect with you, on the one hand, and how simple it is to choose to limit what you share and with whom you share on the other hand. When you choose to follow new people, you can see who follows them, and often, you can see who that person has chosen to follow. (And by "follow," I'm talking about the act of opting to receive updates from someone inside of Google+.)

Facebook and LinkedIn are somewhat more closed. If I'm not your Facebook friend, you have to make special effort to see what I share on my wall. If we're not connected via LinkedIn, you don't receive updates from me. Twitter is more like Google+ from an inclusivity perspective.

Speculating on the Future

The reason I think that Google+ is the next big thing has less to do with the previous information and much more to do with speculating on where things might go. Google, over the past many years, has created several applications that don't exactly line up logically. I think that with Google+, there is a huge potential to link together some of the disparate things, which can create some useful business applications from that linkage. Following are a few thoughts along those lines:

- Google Places enables businesses to add more information to search results. Integrating Google Places data into a Google+ business page means that your customers and prospects can have more information built into search results from Google, which can drive more potential discovery.

- Google Docs is a decent collaborative application, enabling you to create and share documents, spreadsheets, presentations, and more. Adding the communications, sharing, and distribution powers of Google+ to Google Docs means that in-company workflow and collaboration has a new powerhouse tool.

- Google Calendar added event functionality on top of its existing meeting, appointment, and task functionalities. Posting events as a business inside of Google+ enables integrated scheduling and improved findability of events that matter to your prospects.

- Google Checkout is Google's payment solution, which competes with PayPal and Amazon Payments, to name a couple. Integrating payment management into Google+ would permit businesses to execute transactions inside this social network without requiring the user to leave the Google+ ecosystem. (People might be more likely to complete a transaction that stays inside the social network.)

- Google's Android mobile platform has many location-aware features, where your Google searches take into account where you're located, and Google+ is built to accept, post, and share location data. Commerce and marketing options are huge in this "buy where you are" system. This isn't so much speculation because the tools are already in place. It's just up to you to use them as such.

- Google Analytics integration with business pages on Google+ means that not only do you understand the analytics of your primary websites, but now you also have visibility into how people on this social network find your information and what they do with it. This improves your ability to move people toward what they want, not only on your primary website, but also on this social network.

- YouTube is already integrated with Google+. As the #2 search engine, this should be interesting to you. Take it a bit further and you can see that using YouTube as part of your business communications and marketing efforts is a powerful tool when coupled with the sharability and social aspects of Google+.

In speculating, risks always exist. I'm not good at predicting the future—to be quite honest. However, because Google has built dozens and dozens of properties that don't immediately go well together, and because Google+ looks more and more like a potential "communications backbone" to all these various touch points, I think there are some big opportunities to consider, and those who are early to use and master Google+ can be best positioned to take advantage of these potential futures as they arise.

Facebook Is Better. Twitter Is Better. LinkedIn Is for Business.

In the first few weeks of Google+, what I saw more than anything else when I started proclaiming how I felt this would be a powerful new social networking tool (and also important to business) was something along these lines: "All my friends are on Facebook, so there's no way Google+ can become the next big social network."

For a lot of people, that's true now. But as I've said earlier and will say often, it was also true that everybody was on AOL back in the '80s. Systems change. Networks change. You're not still rocking your fax marketing program, are you?

Twitter is excellent at providing rapid, real-time information. It's a great source for news people (who have reported repeatedly that Google+ doesn't give them the same benefits as Twitter does). There's a place and a value for Twitter.

LinkedIn is a great business networking tool. Facebook is wonderful for connecting with people. But as mentioned throughout this book, there are reasons why Google+ trumps them for potential business building—at least for most users.

My First Touch with Google+

Let me be clear: I don't work for Google, nor do I have any particular business relationship with them at the time of this writing. Google had nothing official to do with the making of this book; although, I most certainly asked Google+ team members for thoughts and ideas when it was at all possible.

Google+ became available as a limited "field trial" at the beginning of July 2011. I wasn't given any kind of special access. (I know a few folks at Google, but it's not like people shout, "I've gotta tell Chris Brogan about this!" when they invent something. I'm not that guy.) I just signed up when someone sent me an invite, and I started poking around the moment I had a chance.

What I noticed right away was that, because I was starting at zero, I had the chance to think through how I wanted to interact with this social network. I decided against connecting with everybody, and instead, I started to build small, tight circles of value. I grouped people by whether they represented a business value to me, a personal connection, or were people I wanted to follow to learn from. This process felt a bit like organizing books or a DVD collection, or like building playlists in iTunes. I say this in a positive way.

Right away, it was an addiction. I started "sneaking" Google+. If one of my kids ran off to play, I looked back in and started finding new people to connect with, seeking out people I knew at first, and then *surfing* their connections (I've coined this *friendsurfing*) to see who else I should follow.

What I liked was that I suddenly saw more interesting information because my circles were organized according to my interests. If Danny Sullivan from Search Engine Land shared something about how search rankings were altered by Google+, I could read that, experiment with it, comment back and forth, and become informed. If Jacqueline Carly shared her daily "going to Yoga" photo, I could see that and wish her well.

In other words, because I could organize how the information came in to me at a granular level (if I wanted), I could interact in a more nuanced and interactive way and derive more value from the communication.

Later, when my kids were asleep, I'd get back on Google+ and look around. I logged a lot of hours inside Google+. I'd experiment with posting information. I'd share other interesting things I'd come across. In the early days of Google+, a lot of this sharing was information *about* Google+, such as, "Did you know that if you put an underscore around a word like _this_, it comes out looking like *this*?"

As time went on, people started opening up about what their passions were, inside and outside of work, and this drove even deeper connections of value. I say this as a business person, but also as someone who believes that relationship-minded business is far more valuable than transactional business. If you're looking for "quick fix" sales and marketing methods, Google+ might not be the tool, but if you think there's some value in fostering a community of interest, it works really well for that purpose.

This Sounds Like Other Social Networks

Does Google+ look and feel like other social networks? Yes and no. The closest "feel" to how this compares with other social networks is the way that Google+ allows you to connect with people of interest instead of simply with people you already know in some capacity. Unless you protect your tweets (meaning you've set the privacy such that people you're not following can't see what you're saying), Twitter enables people to discover what you're saying, either by learning about you via a retweet (when someone shares your original message) or by being found via a search.

Google+ does a lot to foster this kind of findability—this discoverable feeling. As you're reading this, you might be thinking, "Facebook does this already." You might say, "LinkedIn is much more businesslike."

But it's different. Google+ is more "open" than Facebook. It is more "deep" than Twitter. It's more rounded than LinkedIn, in that it shows off your personal interests along side your business interests, depending on what you choose to share and post. And, as a business person and a marketer, I saw immediate value in what Google+ can do for your business.

Why Is Google+ So Interesting?

Let me be clear: I'm not usually in the "oh shiny!" tribe. I'm a fan of business and business communication. I love tools that improve business, and especially what I call "human business," which means that it's relationship-minded and yet sustainable. I'm not a "kumbaya" kind of person in that I think, "Let's enjoy everything and keep it free and let's be in a commune together." I have mouths to feed, and when I evaluate a new technology, it's often through the lens of "how can this grow my business?"

Social media and social networks are powerful tools to connect people. Period. This is true, no matter the motive. This works for big businesses I've spent time with, such as General Motors, Pepsico, and Microsoft. Social media and social networks are great for small businesses such as AJ Bombers (burgers) and Glynne Soaps. It works well for solo businesses, such as Joel Libava, the "Franchise King," and Carrie Wilkerson, the Barefoot Executive. Google+ is a great tool for accomplishing all of this.

Google+ is so interesting because it's tied to the number 1 and number 2 search engines in the world (Google and YouTube, respectively). It's interesting because the sharing patterns in there reveal (even without any complicated tools) how information moves, who cares about it, and who's connected to it. With just a handful of clicks and some note-taking, you can see who cared (or didn't care) about the unveiling of a new car.

Speaking of cars, I saw Scott Monty from Ford on Google+ on the second day it was open to the public. I asked Scott why he jumped on Google+ right away:

> "This is the first time we've truly been able to watch a social network being born, and it's kind of like watching the birth of a rare wild animal or a star in another galaxy. The difference between other networks that were born from within is that Google already has a vast presence across the web: platforms and services for mail, calendar, search, analytics, e-commerce, blogging, video, photo, IM, voice, etc., so that Google+ has the potential of being a connector between them all, allowing you to seamlessly move from one to the next, all while connected to the network. For businesses, the attractiveness of Google+ is the prospect of being able to deliver highly relevant content that is tailored specifically to consumers."

The Sharing Culture Grows and Grows

Over the last few years, sharing and self-reporting have become a way of life for hundreds of millions of people. We use social media and social networks to give opinions, to seek advice, to report on our experience. A few scant years ago, it would have seemed strange to take a picture of your food at a restaurant. But wow, how the times have changed.

For example, I was at Legal Sea Foods in Boston one night and my server delivered my order of bourbon lobster to the table. When she put it down, she said, "Nice, huh? Take a picture!" So, I did. I shared it on Google+ and within 10 minutes, I had seventy comments about lobster.

This is a relatively new thing, this sharing of daily moments. Some of it is frivolous and silly, and yet, it's in those moments that serendipity takes over and business value can happen. I'll tell you another story that explains that.

I once sent a tweet that said the following: "If I think the Cadillac CTS is sexy, does that make me an old man?" I got about 200 replies over the span of 30 minutes. (For the record, about 198 people said it didn't make me an old man.) What I didn't expect, however, was that someone from GM would see the tweet, would see the replies, would take an interest, and then would invite me to GM headquarters to meet with the guy responsible for the Cadillac CTS.

This meeting would've been cool if it stopped there, but it didn't. I ended up getting to meet Fritz Henderson, then chairman of General Motors. Think about that: I'm a blogger and small business owner. I'm not the kind of guy the chairman of a huge auto manufacturer gives 30 minutes of his day to, for nothing more than a chat about how social media is reshaping things. The benefits of that meeting and other interactions continue to resonate to this day.

The culture of sharing is a strange one, and it's not immediately apparent how this translates to business, but I can tell you that it does. It happens all the time, and almost always from serendipitous interactions.

When I talk about social media, I like to say this: "Social media is like a multifaceted phone, mixed with an awkward television, mixed with a publishing and media company." What I mean is that you can use it to communicate, to consume interesting content, and to share information with a larger potential audience than what is traditionally available to the average business person. This culture of sharing is what makes using Google+ both challenging and ultimately rewarding.

Another Social Network to Manage? Really?

I hear this often: "*Another* social network to manage? *Really*?" The word "really" in this outcry is often as long and whiny as a teenager being told they can't go out on Thursday night.

Don't think like that. Unless you're still managing your AOL page and your Prodigy profile, it's quite likely that you've moved from one social network to another over the last 3 to 5 years. Are you still active on MySpace? Justin Timberlake's rescue mission notwithstanding, I think that's a risky venture, given the stats.

So yes, I'm telling you that you need to consider and get on Google+, and you have to do it now. You might not need to open up shop and be fully engaged in Google+ as a social media outpost just yet, but you should at least have a few personal profiles built and work to understand the way people interact on the service.

What Do People Do on Google+?

People do a handful of baseline activities on Google+, as explained from a business-minded perspective.

- **Fill out your profile:** A blend of Google's previous Profile functionality, now married to Google+. You can add location data, contact data, links to whatever URLs matter to you, photos, videos, and much more. Not filling out a profile on Google+ as a business professional is like handing out blank rectangles of cardboard and calling them business cards.

- **Organize circles:** How Google+ enables you to organize who you follow, who you share with, and who can see certain posts. If I add you to a circle, I'm giving you permission to see something that I post. If you haven't chosen to follow me back, you won't see my posts, even though I've added you. Circles, in the business sense, enable you to message people internally and externally in different ways, and it's a powerful concept, after you get it set up.

- **Post:** People share information about themselves (photos, video, text, links, and location data) and about what interests them. You can post pictures of new products or a video tour of your new restaurant, for instance.

- **Share:** Other people post interesting things. If it relates to your constituents, you can share their posts with people in your circles of connections. If you're a real estate agent in Austin, Texas, you might share upcoming events that locals post. You might share school news or anything else that ups the "community" feel for the people you court for business.

- **Comment/Plus:** Located below posts and appear in the order they were submitted. You can type out a reply, share a link, or just press the +1 button to indicate that you agree with the sentiment of a post. (Subsequently, you can also +1 other people's comments, showing that you agree with them.) Commenting might be as simple as answering a customer complaint and helping that person find the easiest way to get a swift resolution. You might also comment on your own posts, answering questions from people who've taken the time to comment.

- **Hangouts:** A powerful video chat feature. It enables up to 10 users simultaneously to talk back and forth on video. Michael Dell has already started looking into ways to use Hangouts as a way for Dell to interact with customers. Others use it for simple collaboration among team members.

- **Chat:** Google+ takes Google Talk's chat and integrates it into the sidebar. You can use it as an instant messenger client, and as an open chat room with your circles. (This is how Google+ enables you to organize the people you choose to share information with.) If you've used any kind of instant messenger or chat client, you know how this works.

These are the main functions people interact with on Google+. If it sounds a lot like what you can do on Facebook, LinkedIn, or Twitter, you're not entirely wrong. From a technical standpoint, the experience feels *cleaner* in Google+, in that it works better, and it is structured for a more inclusive feel (if you're not already following me and I post something to the general public, you're much more likely to find it than on other social networks), and these add up to *some* of what makes me so bullish on Google+.

So, with this chapter as your backdrop, you can get into Google+ to see how it can help power your business. Along the way, we'll talk about some of the how-to aspects, but more often, we'll discuss the why-to parts and what you can do to take advantage of this powerful social platform. You'll do some step-by-step things from time to time, but that will be the exception and not the rule. You can pick up that information simply with just a few Google searches. I'd rather share the good stuff, if that works for you.

Google+ Ghost Town: One for the Naysayers

At the time of this writing, Google+ has over 400 million users. That's double and then some what it had when I wrote the first edition of this book. Yet, engagement is decidedly lagging behind other platforms, at least when it comes to business and brand interactions. Because of repeated posts and complaints from people about the sense that not as much is going on here, people are having a harder time digging into this network. The reason for this section is to address the naysayers, to acknowledge some of the current state, and to tell you why you should form your own opinion.

The Average Isn't All That It Seems

According to a blog post citing research from RJ Metrics,[1] in a sampling of 40,000 users of Google+, the average replies per post is one. The average +1 per post is the same. The average time between posts is 12 days. It sounds dismal, but these numbers are where my first rebuttal comes in.

The word "average" is the key. Yes, the platform isn't bustling all over the place for every user, but there are many interactions happening and all kinds of engagement. On the day I wrote this, I looked at a post on the Ford Motor Company account asking for a single word to describe a picture of one of their cars. There were 170 responses. Intel sees a more modest dozen comments per post. Starbucks sees a dozen or more comments. NASA posted a picture of the blue moon that happened right after the death of astronaut Neil Armstrong, and it received more than 500 comments, 1,300 shares, and 3,750 +1s.

These examples are the first indicators of something to note. How does NASA get that kind of response when other big-name companies aren't quite there yet? It may well be that the early adopter tech-centric crowd simply will get more attention than the less tech-minded brands and companies over the next handful of months.

What People Are Saying and What It Might Mean to You

What exactly are people saying about the stats and numbers, and what should it mean to you as you make a decision about whether to use Google+ or join the naysayers? The following sections take a look.

Google+ Is Still Skewing a Bit Tech Nerd

I've argued in the past that it's not so, that Google+ isn't just for the cutting-edge crowd, but the stats point to *engagement* happening in the "cutting edge" community more than any others. For example, if I look at comments on posts by *The Boston Globe*, there are five to ten per post most days. Comments to *Wired Magazine*? Hundreds for most posts. Starbucks? A dozen comments. Think Geek has 30 to 50. The engagement is most definitely skewed toward the early adopters.

Remember That Engagement Is Only One Measurement

In my role as advisor to larger companies, I'm often asked to help make sense of digital media metrics and what they mean for a business. The question asked is how to track the dollar value of something such as a Facebook like or a +1. The answer is that there's no direct dollar correlation. It's not the same as the metrics of direct mail or email marketing, where you can track the numbers in your audience, open rate, click rate, and so on. Instead, it's a rough measure to say, "This many people liked this information enough to potentially share it." Beyond that, one might extrapolate that something shared a lot more than something else improves "awareness," but that rarely tracks to revenue.

This becomes a bit complex to explain to the senior team. If you're a marketing manager and you're trying to justify the time spent on Google+, and you show them a post with two comments and a few pluses, it's unlikely that you're going to wow them. Instead, you have to be able to show other metrics. Here are some potential examples:

- Percentage of conversation shares (measured by tools such as Salesforce Radian6).

- Click rate of links (make a specific link for G+ versus other avenues and count that in Google Analytics or your analytics package).

- Revenue (my favorite). If you're getting buyers, who cares if they are hitting the +1 button?

Sharing Is Still the Question at Hand

According to a survey from MediaBistro,[2] for every 100 million users on a social network, 197 users are likely to share a story on Twitter (which has far fewer users than Google+ or Facebook), 41 users are likely to share via Facebook, 15 via LinkedIn, and only 6 on Google+. Equalized out for numbers of users, Google+ is by far the least-shared-into network right now.

Engagement is certainly the biggest complaint for brands. In another survey,[3] brands like Coca-Cola pointed out that they have 2,500 +1s on Google+ compared to 46 million likes on Facebook. IBM has 6,900 +1s to 143,000 likes. Even Google itself has 1.1 million +1s and 10.3 million likes.

The rebuttal? The sharing buttons for Google+ are far less ubiquitous on websites that use social sharing at present. If something is easier for users to do, that's what they'll choose. Does this mean the data is skewed? No. The data reports accurately that not as many people are sharing into Google+ as other networks. But to me, this is a matter of some site updates more than it's a matter of something systemic. If you want more people to share your content on Google+, put up a button to share it.

The Vampire Problem

Google+ was developed to be a lot easier to use than Facebook, to let users manage their own privacy better than Facebook, and to promote a much more at-your-request level of interaction with brands than how one experiences Facebook. This last point is another part of why brands and businesses are having an issue with gaining traction with Google+. I call it the vampire problem.

In vampire movies (and some legends), a vampire isn't permitted into your home until you invite him or her. As a brand on Google+, a personal account has to circle your brand page before you can initiate a conversation with that user. Think about the difference in the barriers.

On Facebook, you just click Like and, oh, we'll fill the sidebar with stuff your friends like, and we'll give the brand as much data as we have on you just because you clicked Like. On Google+, you circle the brand just like you do a friend, and then that brand has the capability to interact with you on Google+. On Google+, a brand ends up acting more at the same interaction level as a friend once you circle it, whereas a brand liked on Facebook shows up in many more ways as part of the advertising efforts of that platform.

It's not too difficult to understand why it's a little harder to get businesses excited about interacting with people on Google+. However, to look at it the other way, as stated previously, it's a lot more civil and user-friendly to consider how Google+ built these interactions. It's like the old conversation about spam (not the meat but the unwanted mail). It's targeted marketing when you send it, but it's spam if you receive it. You can argue either side, but technically, it's nicer if the users have a say over whether or not they chit chat with you marketer types.

The API Problem

The real problem for people as it's been reported to me is that access to the API (application programming interface) isn't available at the time of this writing, nor has it been for over a year. Some companies are working on trials with it, but it's not exactly out there for all third parties to build into. By comparison, Twitter launched and released that access a few months later, and Facebook made their technology available relatively quickly as well (though not as quickly as Twitter).

The lack of an API limits all kinds of activities that we're used to in other social networks, including the following:

- Having more than one choice of social media posting client

- Scheduled posts

- Listening tool integration (tools such as Radian6 can't integrate with Google+ yet)

- Third-party value adds

Without this, Google+ can't hope to acquire more traction and more of a market share. The company can encourage people onto the platform, but if it's difficult to interact with the platform, users will get discouraged. By contrast, for instance, tools like Hootsuite can schedule posts across Twitter, Facebook, and LinkedIn. I can add Foursquare and even MySpace, but for Google+, currently, I'm limited to administrating my pages but not my primary account. This is the challenge. With no capability to potentially schedule posts, with very limited use of tools to add in other technologies, people are reacting accordingly.

Why I'm Still Betting on Google+

Following is a version of the same thing I say every time someone asks me about whether he or she should invest in Google+ for their business:

- Google+ is linked heavily to the #1 search engine in the world: Google.

- Google+ is linked heavily to the #2 search engine in the world: YouTube.

- Google+ is linked heavily to Google Local (see Figure 1-1).

- Google+ feeds organic search engine information in Google.

- Google+ is tied heavily into Android, which has a growing market share of the mobile and tablet market.

- Increasingly, Google links Google+ into more of its other services, requiring one to use a Google+ account to interact, but also permitting a rich interaction.

Figure 1-1   Google+ meets Google Local.

These pluses trump the complaints about not being able to find friends. For one thing, posting to "Public" on Google+ creates organic search material that's useful whether someone engages with you on Google+ or not. Meaning, what you say in public impacts what people find in Google search. Thus, if you're writing about the "best burgers in Milwaukee," and you mention AJ Bombers, it's likely that it'll help my friend Joe when someone uses Google to search for "best burgers in Milwaukee." Make sense?

Even if you don't know a lot about search engine optimization (I sure don't), you can swing by Google and put in the name of a local business or type of business. If a business has a Google Places listing, it gets much better visibility than other types of listings. Now that this has been integrated tightly into Google+, it's a no-brainer to work on populating the new Google+ Local pages and make them work for you. By the way, to list your business on Google Local, go here: www.google.com/local/add.

With YouTube, the quality of comments is far lower than what you get on Google+. If you're working hard on creating great content, why not put it somewhere that the comments might equal the quality of your work? Not that comments pay the bills, but they're certainly a better feedback mechanism.

As I mentioned, Google+ is tied into Android, Google's mobile operating system. You might not pay attention to something as obscure as mobile operating system trends. In a report dated August 2012,[4] IDC reported that Google's Android OS accounted for 68.1 percent of all smartphones sold. Apple owns a little over 16 percent of the OS market, which should make you pause a moment, given that most people are surprised because of how ubiquitous the iPhone *seems* out in the wild.

Compare that to Facebook, which has no mobile operating system. Yes, Facebook is used actively on both Android and iOS phones, and there are more people using it than Google+ or Twitter on those smartphones, but let's say it again in slow motion: Google owns the operating system of more than two-thirds of the smartphones and they've moved to tie Google+ deep into that operating system. Whether or not all your friends are on Facebook, it's fairly difficult to imagine Google (one of the wealthiest companies in the world) failing to implement even more action on a well-distributed platform.

The story is a little different when it comes to tablets,[5] with one source pointing out that based on usage (not ownership), Apple's iOS is responsible for more than 85 percent of worldwide Internet access on tablets versus only 13 percent for Android. But even there, I'll use this to say that none of these devices are built or powered by Facebook.

Throughout this book, I point out that I don't consider the fight to be Google+ versus Facebook. I will say it again here. My point in bringing up Facebook is that when I mention all the potential for Google+, the first thing out of everyone's mouth is why Facebook will dominate throughout the rest of history, even as its stock crumbles in the public marketplace and even though two of the wealthiest companies in the world dominate the growing mobile device marketplace.

My role in the business world over the past decade has been a multifaceted one. I've consulted with and spoken to the leadership and teams of several of the world's largest companies. I've spent time with Microsoft, Coca-Cola, General Motors, and many other companies. We usually talk about how one might use various aspects of these digital tools for business purposes. I have never ever thought of myself as much of a futurist, though I do spend a lot of time helping people vector their best efforts against "what comes next."

The reason I've been so drawn to Google+ since its launch is that I believe there are many forces that have a chance of adding to the potential for a big shift in how social networks impact business. Because Google "owns" the search category at present (how people discover your business) and because Google owns the mobile OS category (the underpinnings of your mobile device) and Google's web browser Chrome is currently out front in the web browser race (by only a slim margin, but still), and because Google has lots of money to throw at this from an advertising standpoint, I think it will shift how social networks impact businesses.

Some people have asked whether I was paid by Google to promote Google+, and the answer is no. Boy, that would make a great gig, but no. Others have said that I'm defending Google+ because I wrote a book about it, and I will look foolish if it fails. That's a reasonable opinion, but I'm quite willing to look foolish without making the effort to write an entire book. Instead, I will finish by pointing out that history has a way of repeating itself. Empires fall. Google+ has launched at the same point that Facebook is about to hit an apex in its distribution. If nothing else, I'm playing the safe bet by voting on Google+ as the next big thing for businesses in the social network game. But that's for you to decide.

Endnotes

1. http://sproutsocial.com/insights/2012/05/google-plus-engagement-low/

2. http://www.mediabistro.com/alltwitter/google-plus-ghost-town_b26573

3. http://www.digiday.com/brands/top-brands-lonely-on-google-plus/

4. http://www.engadget.com/2012/08/08/idc-android-and-ios-continue-to-carve-up-the-world-another-rec/

5. http://royal.pingdom.com/2012/07/31/state-of-the-tablet-market/

The Opportunity of Google+

On the Google earnings call in July 2011, Larry Page reported that 20 million people were using Google+ within the first few weeks. This was Google's version of a "limited" field trial, by the way. When I talk about this statistic, people tend to come back and say, "Yeah, but Google already had a huge user base in its other products, and you can't compare it to Facebook, which started off as a service for colleges only, or Twitter, which was a startup." That's not what I'm talking about.

What I'm talking about is that there were already 20 million users within the first few weeks, meaning that the service will quickly be viable as a social network. The issue with social networks from a business perspective is that you must wonder (and worry) about whether your prospective buyers, vendors, and customers actually use the network, and you must find out how easy or difficult it is to reach them. People care about numbers in this regard.

In contrast to Google+'s user base in July 2011, Facebook had approximately 750 million users. That means that 1 in 11 people on the planet have a Facebook account. The immediate reaction that I get when talking about how Google+ might become the predominant social network choice for business users is that Facebook is so much bigger.

In the '80s, AOL was much bigger than Facebook—because Facebook didn't exist. Years later, Friendster was all the rage. In 2005, MySpace was the place to be. And yes, Google+ will likely vanish at some point, just like Facebook might vanish at some point. Whenever someone says something is here to stay, it's easy to point out thousands of examples (especially online) of social networks and other services that were huge and then faded away.

But consider one huge difference: Google+ is a social network built by the company that's held the rank of the #1 search engine for years and years. YouTube is the #2 search engine—and Google owns YouTube. By contrast, Facebook doesn't even permit Google to index its content. At the time of this writing, Facebook dwarfs Google+ as a user base. The thing to keep your eye on is that search is how people find your business, and the #1 search engine in the world now pays close attention to what people do on Google+. If that doesn't get your eyebrows raised and make you lean forward, I'm not sure what will.

Where Google+ Fits in the Business Ecosystem

Where does Google+ fit in the business ecosystem? This is harder to answer than you might think because that's like answering the question, "Where does the phone fit in the business ecosystem?" Ask a salesperson, and he would say that Google+ is about nurturing prospects at the wide edge of the sales funnel. Ask a customer service or community person and she would say Google+ is a great community management tool. A PR or marketing professional would see this tool as great for business communications and awareness efforts. Someone focused on internal communications would say it is a collaboration tool.

All those answers are correct. How you want to use Google+ for your business is up to you. Many opportunities are worth consideration. It depends on how willing you are to adapt to using the tools, and it matters how you integrate the tools into the rest of your workflow. To that point, now look at some of the opportunities that Google+ offers.

Google+ Opportunities

Following are some of the many ways to use Google+ for your business:

- **Collaboration:** You can make a circle of coworkers and business colleagues and easily share information with them. This is a circle in which you probably wouldn't share anything that is too personal, such as the fact you got your dog fixed or you're having trouble making your mortgage payment. In business cases, you obviously wouldn't share sensitive data in a public setting (even if there are privacy settings that "should" protect you). The tools for collaboration inside of Google+ are intuitive, offer many potential modes of interaction, and allow for strong communication options. You can send textual information with your team, point to links, share photos or videos, and use the Hangout feature to have live conversations with your team.

- **Learning:** This isn't just a site for the bleeding-edge techies. All kinds of interesting communities have formed on Google+. Thousands of photography enthusiasts and professionals find the value to share photos and talk about their trade. Financial professionals share ideas and give insight into what motivates them. This platform offers all kinds of ways to learn.

- **Discovery:** Google+ has become the #1 traffic driver to my website, www.chrisbrogan.com. Your results may vary, but I'm pointing this out because it means that people are suddenly discovering my site via this social network, and that means it's a lead generator for you to consider.

- **Community Building:** Comic writer Greg Pak uses Google+ to share updates about his projects and event information so that people can connect with him at events, and get sneak previews of projects he's working on. I've seen people use this successfully many times as a way to grow their influence and awareness well beyond what traditional media outlets typically permit. It allows you a kind of blend between a publishing platform and a powerful new kind of telephone. You can do the same community building as a business if you take the time to actively participate in communities and engage customers and prospects in two-way interactions.

- **Contests and Promotions:** Yes, it's old school marketing, but that doesn't mean it's not effective. iPad2 giveaways, photo caption contests, and all kinds of other engaging experiences take place, and early reports from those who've conducted these contests are quite positive.

- **Customer Service:** As I mentioned in Chapter 1 ("How Did I Get Here?") Michael Dell from Dell Corporation has started to test Google+ as a customer service channel. This doesn't replace your company's call center, but there have already been many companies that use Twitter as another customer service channel. The potential return on investment (ROI) and customer approval/satisfaction improvements are huge.

- **Engagement:** Your main website is built for a specific purpose, plus it's *your* "real estate." You might not be as free to talk "off-topic" there, and you might have specific goals that preclude you from engaging in two-way conversations on that site. For instance, if you're running a website that sells plumbing supplies, it might not be a good idea to post your appreciation of the *Family Guy* TV show. However, sharing something personal in a place like Google+ helps round out a prospective customer's perception of you and enables you to talk about something not directly related to selling from time to time. Because your main site is your "home base," Google+ makes a great "outpost" that enables you to engage with people, talk off-topic, learn more about your prospective buyers and community, and build relationships outside of the sales funnel. This level of engagement gets touted a lot in all books about social media, but it's worth repeating—it is a huge opportunity.

- **Listening:** For years, I've been saying that listening is "the new black." The ability to search the web to find what people are saying about you, your products, your competitors, and more, is the best part of what social media and social networks deliver. Because Google thoroughly indexes the information in Google+, you have the built-in opportunity to pay attention to what people say, and then you can reach out and make contact with some of these people, should that prove useful to your business goals.

- **Referrals:** One way to get great value from Google+ is to seek and offer referrals. Imagine you sell custom sneakers, such as Heyday Footwear does, and you run a web-based business instead of a brick-and-mortar one. For instance, if you're Heyday Footwear, you can post pictures and maybe videos showing the designs you're currently working on. You can invite the audience to interact and comment on the process. Getting involvement definitely helps. Now, imagine asking previous buyers of such custom footwear to post photos and maybe videos talking about how much they love their new shoes. Now, you've got the opportunity to see referrals and testimonials come in from your audience, which is even more powerful than anything you'll ever say about your own products.

- **Sharing:** The most powerful opportunity in Google+ is sharing. If you are fortunate, people will interact with the information you post and share it with *their* audiences.

Preparing Yourself for Opportunity

One of the first things I noticed when I joined Google+ is that many people didn't do much with the About page of their profile. I learned a while back from best-selling author Marsha Collier that your Google Profile page is a kind of "secret" way to make some potential connections that might otherwise have slipped past you. The new profile options inside of Google+ really improve your ability to make potential relationships and grow your business, but only if you take the time to prepare yourself to receive opportunities.

Consider the following three main points when setting up your Google+ profile page to use it to its best advantage:

- The more people who can understand about how to work with you from what you've written, the more likely they'll take the next step to connect with you.

- The more thoroughly you fill out your profile, the more opportunities you have to connect with people who see something there that matches their needs.

- The easier you make it for people to contact you via that Profile page, the more likely you can turn a browser into a prospect.

One of the best ways to move someone from "interested in what you're sharing and posting" to "interested in what you're selling" is to make those connections and transition points easy.

Here are a few other tips to keep in mind to prepare yourself for opportunity:

- Keep your circles well organized. This might seem like a chore at first, but the more granular you keep your circles, the better the chance you'll see something of specific value flow by in your stream.

- Build outbound circles. Chapter 6, "Circles," talks about how to build outbound circles, but different from how you organize the people you want to follow and observe, an outbound circle is a list of people you want to share specific kinds of information with. For instance, I have an outbound circle called "Press," where I share information that reporters and other news professionals might find useful. I have another called "MKTG" for web entrepreneurs, who want some specific tactics and tips on how to use Google+ for more business. Your outbound circles might be different, but the concept is the same.

- Share links back to your main website or blog, but sparingly. People who have you in their circles want to know about you, but they also want you to be a source of other people's good information. The more you talk about yourself, the more people tune out. It's like a cocktail party. You can post and share relevant information as much as you'd like (though too much might get you uncircled by others, meaning they'll stop seeing your updates), but you should consider a blend, anywhere from 5 of other people's items to every one of yours or perhaps closer to 10 to 1.

- Build your use of Google+ into your schedule. It's not like your day job is to interact on social networks (unless it is). Consider posting information and shares two times a day, and consider dipping in to answer comments and talk back and forth at least two times a day, as well. The more interaction you have on Google+ (beyond just posting and sharing), the more opportunity you have to find potential business relationships.

- Think up ways to use Hangouts, the live video chat feature. Aaron Manley Smith of Motorphilia uses Hangouts for virtual Bible study. You can limit attendance to a hangout to those members of a circle, or you can invite the public at large to participate in a free-for-all video chat. Both have their advantages.

The Personal Touch and Personality

Sometimes, especially when talking with larger corporations, I'm asked whether it's a good idea to share personal information and topics that might not be germane to your primary business focus. Ask yourself this question right now: Do you prefer buying from someone pushing a sales agenda, or do you prefer buying from someone you feel understands you or you feel you understand?

Several reports and studies over the years boil down to the same thing: We buy from people we like. Though this isn't *always* an option, it's more common that we, as buyers, will bend our justifications around going with the choice that supports this view.

For example, think about your experience with restaurants near where you live or work. When you go to a place and feel warmly welcomed, that experience makes you more likely to revisit. The more you revisit, the more you feel "known" and valued. Sometimes, this comes from sharing stories with a server. Other times, it comes from the staff knowing something about you and your preferences.

Now, translate this to the online world. When people get the opportunity to learn more about who you are and what matters to you, they find reasons to be more interested in your other business pursuits, and this can come from all kinds of wild and varied angles.

Your personality can shine on a social network like Google+, and this will help with business-building. How do you do it? You talk about things related to your business, but you also talk about other points of interest outside of your day job. It's a balancing act because if someone is coming to you to learn about your passion for education, and you end up sharing more on Google+ about your passion for reality TV shows, the disconnect might not really help you grow your business. But it can be done.

Consider this your litmus test: Would you talk to someone about this while waiting in line for something? If yes, then it's probably okay to talk about in an off-topic way as a means to sharing more of your personality. If no, then don't share it on Google+.

Blending Business and Personal

Start with this disclaimer: If you share all kinds of weird intimate details about how your life is a shambles, how you hate cats, or endless streams of nonsensical "chatter," it probably won't benefit your business. A certain element of curation is required for how you choose to share your personal thoughts and ideas alongside your business information. Filter yourself a little, to be sure that you're not turning away any potential business connections. Pick and choose between all the thoughts that rush into your head, and maybe don't post each and every one of them to your stream on Google+. By "curation," the idea is that you are your own mental editor, and you pick the "best of" your thoughts and ideas for the day to share with people.

But you'd be surprised by what causes a connection.

Following are some of the stranger things I've shared that have brought me unexpected connections:

- My appreciation of '90s hip-hop music
- Photos of the lake and waterfall near my house
- My love of Batman (and comics in general)
- A single tweet about a car
- Random one-liner jokes
- Reports on my efforts to get more fit
- A photo of a lobster

In all the previous cases, those random choices to share have resulted in an increase in my follower base, and in all those cases, it led to a business relationship that eventually ended in financial and strategic worth. Re-read that list. It's absolutely silly. And yet, because I blend business information (mine and sharing great stuff from other people), people start to feel like they know me. We buy from people we like, and we like people we feel we know.

Start Early

I joined Twitter in 2006 and was one of the first 10,000 or so users. Twitter gave me a platform that translated into quite a lot of business value. People who came to Twitter much later didn't always meet with the same success. I believe that my choice to learn as much as I could about the platform and to use it heavily to build relationships was part of what led to my business success.

The same can be true for Google+. The sooner you get in, start, and build some relationships of value, the better your chances to have a first-mover advantage.

Don't worry that it's early days. Consider this a great opportunity to get the jump on others who prefer to wait and see what comes of new platforms like this. Scott Monty, head of social media for Ford Motor Company, was on Google+ on day 2. To me, that speaks volumes about him really understanding the value of Ford starting early, and it gives you further proof that you should consider doing the same.

This service isn't yet widely available to the public, and invitations are required, but if you ask your web-savvy friend for an invite, chances are they'll have one. At some point, this service will be open to the public, but if you wait that long, you'll miss the boat.

The sooner you get into the game, the sooner you can use the tools to change how you grow your business. It also enables you to experiment faster, make more mistakes faster (before more people are there), and have a presence before some of your competitors.

What You Can Accomplish with Google+

Everyone reads books (especially business books) with a specific goal in mind: "What's in it for me?" That's okay. If you're going to spend your time and money on a business book, there should be some value given in the exchange. But one of the most important things about how to use Google+—and social networks in general—is to learn how to build value by promoting and helping others.

In 2009, Julien Smith and I said in our book, *Trust Agents*, "Be the elbow of every deal." What we meant was that there's great value and long-term influence in helping others make connections and build business relationships. Without ever asking for reciprocation, this one move of helping others connect and make business happen with no immediate value to you is a power move worth mastering.

In Google+, you can do this in several ways. One is by sharing posts from people with smaller audiences. Another is to make introductions between two people you follow who might not yet follow others. Another is to promote products and services that aren't yours but that would help your constituency. These are all big opportunities to build value for others and build relationships in general.

In opposition to "What's in it for me," consider, "What can I do for others that can help them?" What this brings you, if executed in earnest, is a lot of respect and admiration from people in your community, and if one were to be honest, that kind of currency translates well into people's willingness to share your content with others, with their interest in participating with you and your posts, and with people's perception of you and your motives. Don't do one simply to earn the other, but understand that, should you work toward this mindset, it does indeed pay off in tangible dividends, even if these aren't always directly monetary in nature.

Opportunity Is What You Make of It

Google+ isn't a hardcore sales and marketing engine. The game, such as it is, isn't to get the most followers and then start blasting them with offers until they purchase. It is, instead, a way to educate prospective buyers, a way to connect with your community of customers, a method by which to promote offers and events (sparingly) to your audience, and a way to build relationships before you need them.

If you've noticed, a lot of these methods and means aren't exactly hardcore tricks and tactics yet, which is explored in later chapters. The reason I start with this talk about potential opportunity and about the mindset behind what might be helpful for you, and all this stress on relationship-minded business practices, is that these are what are required for a mindset before you dig deep into the heavier selling or other business functions. I hope that works for you.

We've talked about what you *can* do and why you might do it, and we've talked about a lot of the various methods by which you can find opportunities in Google+. The next chapter walks you through several "serving suggestions." Pick up a can of vegetable soup at the grocery store, and you'll see a picture on the outside of the can with the words "serving suggestion" nearby. What they mean by that is, "Hey! You can make what's in this can look like this picture, if you want."

Now do that with Google+ by creating a few potential recipes for how professionals might use it for different businesses.

A Day in the Life

I'm writing this book in the early days of the launch of Google+, so my interviews with business professionals on how this platform integrates into their day is based on a scant few weeks of experience and effort. Even so, kernels of possibility are wrapped up in what I discovered in their answers and their current methods. Further, in all cases, the people interviewed blended the answer to what they do with Google+ into the overall sense of what they do with all the other social software platforms they currently employ for business purposes.

What follows are a bunch of recipes. Starting with myself, but then going immediately into interviews with people from all levels of business and in a variety of industries, I have put together some "serving suggestions" for you to consider in deciding how you want to use Google+ for your own business value. You see that many ways exist to use the platform, and some people prefer to use it one way, whereas others have a different perspective on the value of the platform. This was done intentionally.

There's no one right way to use this tool. Some people post a lot of original material but don't choose to curate or share much. Others are hubs for sharing but don't create a lot of original material. Still others spend a lot of time reading and posting in the comments section and some people use Google+ as just another source of information to read and consider.

To call any one use of the platform wrong (barring outright spamming and bullying) is to limit the possibilities that you might find in using Google+ in ways that provide value for your needs. Why should I (or anyone) tell you that you're doing it wrong, if you're getting something useful out of your method? To that end, read through some of the ways people use Google+ with an open mind, and think about whether you can borrow from several of their experiences to form your own.

My Personal Day in the Life of Google+

I should preface this part by saying that my business is quite varied. I consult and speak for large companies, and I create products and services for small businesses. That juxtaposition makes it hard to nail down how I use Google+ for my business pursuits, but I'm game to explain it, just the same. Following is a summary of how I use it:

Time Used per Day: 2 hours (This is part of my primary job.)

Primary Goals of Usage: Build an audience, convert to community, and drive awareness for projects or topics of interest

Number of Original Posts per Day: 6 (average)

Number of Shared Posts per Day: 8 or more (average)

Number of Comments per Day: This varies. If I'm traveling, there are fewer. If I'm not traveling, 20–30 comments on average.

Links to My Blog or Projects per Day: 2 (average)

Number of Off-Topic Posts per Day: 3 (I added this to show that there's value in writing about things that aren't pertinent to your main business. The mileage varies for this stat, especially because my business is a little more diverse than most.)

Typical Strategy: Because my goals are to build an audience, convert them to a community, and then drive awareness to my projects or other topics of interest, I read bits of the streams from my various circles, posting what I think are interesting links, and then commenting back and forth with people on various posts (theirs and my own). And I spend some time promoting my own projects or things that interest me that aren't mine.

I admit that when I have a little free time, or if I'm procrastinating, I tend to read posts for a while to catch up on other interesting (but not necessarily important to my business) posts shared by others. Sometimes, this serendipitous consumption permits me to build new relationships because I might follow someone's shared post and then learn more about the creator by reading his or her profile—and poof, suddenly, I've added someone else of interest to my circles to follow.

I also use a small, limited pair of circles called Close and Keepers to pay attention to people who matter to me. This lets me dip into those streams to be sure to catch any news that they share, or help with any problems they might have, and that's something that was harder for me to do on Twitter or Facebook, even with list functionality. (For whatever reason, Google+ seems and feels cleaner to me.)

But now, let's move away from me and catch up with others. I've chosen these people to interview for a few reasons. In all cases, I either knew the person, or I got to know them via Google+. In all cases, these people represent different ways to use Google+, which is a great way to represent ways *you* might consider using the platform for your day-in-the-life experiences.

Interview with Scott Monty, Ford Motor Company

Scott Monty is the head of social media for Ford Motor Company. We've been friends for years, as Scott started his rise to prominence in the Boston area where I'm from. Over the years, Scott has led and participated in several innovative projects. I saw him all over Google+ on the second day it was open, and therefore, I knew he'd be the right person to ask about how someone in one of the top three auto makers in the United States uses Google+ for business.

Time Used per Day: 1 hour

Primary Goals of Usage: Surface interesting content, build relationships, share experiences, learn

Number of Original Posts per Day: 3–5

Number of Shared Posts per Day: 2–3

Number of Comments per Day: 10–12

Links to My Blog or Projects per Day: 1

Number of Off-Topic Posts per Day: 4

Typical Strategy: I've got my circles pretty well defined, so I look first for those in the tech and influencer circles to see what cool and cutting-edge stuff they're sharing. I find that these groups keep me attuned to industry news, changes, and thoughtful, longer content posts. Then I look to friends, acquaintances, and other close circles to see what's on their minds. When I find really good content from a "noisy" person, I'm careful about sharing it with too many other people and contributing to the noise, instead preferring to comment or *+1* it.

Special Uses: Nothing personally, but for the Ford Motor Company account, we use it to share heritage and archival material, as well as Hangouts with otherwise hard-to-reach executives.

Scott's doing a lot in early days to connect and build relationships. He doesn't talk 100% Ford Motor Company, but he definitely represents his brand. I talk about his content strategy in a subsequent chapter, but the thing to learn from Scott is his gentlemanly approach to connecting with people. Remember: His buyer is anyone who drives a car. It's a decent demographic to chase.

Interview with Greg Pak, Comic Book Author and Screen Writer

I knew Greg Pak as an author but not personally, but when I saw a single post of his on Google+, I added him to one of my circles and immediately started closely following his work. I also ran out and bought several of his most recent comic books so that I was "in the know" on what my new "friend" was up to.

That's what is so cool about Google+: There's an instant sense of connectivity that seems to come from using these tools. For example, when Greg shared his schedule of appearances at the San Diego Comicon, and when I commented on how clever that was, he answered back quickly, was human in his interactions, and earned a new fan (and hopefully friend) without a lot of hard work. If you're a creator of any kind, you should think about how Greg talks about his day in the life to see what you can glean from his usage of Google+.

Time Used per Day: 30 minutes to 1 hour

Primary Goals of Usage: Keep current readers aware of what's going on with my projects and books and try to reach and rope in new readers

Number of Original Posts per Day: 4–6

Number of Shared Posts per Day: 2–3

Number of Comments per Day: 3–5

Links to My Blog or Projects per Day: 4–5

Number of Off-Topic Posts per Day: 1–2

Typical Strategy: Because I have comic books coming out every week or two, I tend to have a steady stream of news to share: preview pages, interviews, reminders that books are out, and reviews. At the same time, I keep my eyes open for other news that might be of interest to folks reading my stream—Comixology's 99¢ sales, for example. And I'll reshare interesting posts from folks in my circles, whether they're related to anything I'm working on. The basic idea is to create a familiar voice that readers can trust to share interesting news and discussion, which, of course, just happens to include my own comics work.

I've also made a point to try to thank people for kind comments, answer questions they might have, reshare posts that amuse or enlighten me, and bring the Follow Friday tradition over from Twitter to recommend other interesting people to follow. I'm a big believer in casting your bread upon the water. When you share with others, more comes back to you.

Special Uses: I've done a lot of thinking about digital media, social media, and personal technology over the years—all key themes in my graphic novel *Vision Machine*. So I've found myself using Google+ to talk quite a bit about Google+, which of course is what many users have notoriously spent a huge amount of time doing since the service began. I think that interest in discussing these questions of technology and social media is one of the things that made the service a good match for me from the beginning. I have many friends in the comics field who joined but still haven't posted, probably because few other comics people were posting in the beginning. I was lucky to have an interest in the techy kinds of things that people were discussing in the early weeks, so I had an incentive to stick around and get comfortable.

Moving forward, I'm sure I'll continue to post about technology, social media, and the Google+ experience, which makes sense because it's one of my big areas of interest, but it is also serendipitously a good pull in this specific social network. So I've got that going for me.

The biggest takeaway for business professionals is to see how Greg uses his Google+ stream as a way to share information to connect with his community, and he doesn't limit it to talking about his own work. That's the key. He brings up information that can appeal to the community about their own interests, and you can do the same.

Interview with Jenny Cisney, Kodak's Chief Blogger

Jenny Cisney and I have known each other for a few years, although I mostly know her in her professional capacity as Kodak's Chief Blogger. She's also funny, has a great ability to find interesting things to share, and is the kind of person you feel you already know before having ever met her. Here's how Jenny uses Google+.

Time Used per Day: 1/2 hour to 1 hour

Primary Goals of Usage: Find new, interesting, useful information; share the neat things I find/make/do; and share cool stuff about photography, video, and sharing that can link back to Kodak

Number of Original Posts per Day: 10 (5 personal posts + 5 photography or social media posts)

Number of Shared Posts per Day: 2

Number of Comments per Day: 5

Links to My Blog or Projects per Day: 1 on my personal blog—www.ljcfyi.com—and 1 for Kodak's blog—http://1000words.kodak.com/thousandwords/

Number of Off-Topic Posts per Day: I guess the personal stuff is off topic: 5 personal.

Typical Strategy: Add value to people's lives when it comes to photos, video, printing, and sharing by making it all easier, simpler, and fun. Hopefully our products can do this for them also and they become/remain a happy customer of our brand.

Special Uses: What makes my toe start tapping is the potential for customer support in Google+. How could it play out and how would we support it?

Notes: There is huge potential with Google+, not just via our participation in streams and huddles as a brand, but also in how our products can integrate with it! It's exciting!

Jenny points out one of the facets I am most excited about when thinking of Google+ in a business setting: customer support. Imagine you've just purchased a digital picture frame with Wi-Fi from Kodak, and you can't figure out how your family can email pictures to the frame. In Jenny's view, you could just connect with someone from Kodak on Google+ and explain your issue. Then, the representative from Kodak might invite you into a video Hangout to talk you through the process. It's exciting, for sure.

Interview with Darren Rowse, Problogger

Darren and I have been friends for a few years, even though he lives on nearly the exact opposite side of the planet from me. We connect on most every social network that exists, and we cofounded a membership site, Third Tribe Marketing, with Brian Clark (Copyblogger) and Sonia Simone (Remarkable Blogging) in 2010.

I saw the first published photo of his newest son on Google+, and I've subsequently had several conversations with Darren that I *never* had with him in person, nor on any other social network, including our own private network. Why? Because the platform opened Darren up to being a more rounded individual and not just a professional blogger and digital photographer.

Time Used per Day: 20–60 minutes a day

Primary Goals of Usage: Engagement with readers, testing ideas, building brand, and driving traffic

Number of Original Posts per Day: 3–4

Number of Shared Posts per Day: 3–4

Number of Comments per Day: 20–30

Links to My Blog or Projects per Day: 1–2

Number of Off-Topic Posts per Day: 3–4

Typical Strategy: At this stage I'm experimenting with a variety of types of posts to see what is resonating with readers and to explore what kind of posts work in this new medium. So far I'm trying to mix in a few types of posts each weekday (weekends I tend to go off topic a little more) including the following:

- **Original long-form content:** These posts are either posts from my blog archives from a couple of years back (which I'm refreshing) or they are new posts on things that I'm pondering (which I then often turn into new posts for my blog).

- **Questions:** Asking questions of followers around the topics that I write about either just to generate some discussion or to help me research posts I'm then going to write about.

- **Personal updates:** What I'm doing. Photos from my day, family updates, and so on.

- **Sharing links:** Sharing links to what other people are doing or sharing a link to new posts on my blog. (Although to this point, I'm not sharing links to every new post on my blog—just 1 to 2 per day at a maximum.)

Darren, through his sharing of photos of his family and what he's doing, has kept a personal tone with his community, some of who connect with his Problogger site and others who are members of his Digital Photography School. And yet, he's testing different engagement methods, refreshing old content for a new audience (which is brilliant), and meeting his business goals. This embodies the best way to use Google+ for your business: Drive some awareness and engagement with your primary business focus while showing a personal, humanistic side to your experience.

Interview with Jacqueline Carly, Fitness Professional

Jacqueline Carly is launching Jacq.tv project, an online fitness and nutrition resource for musicians and performers. I think her usage of Google+, starting from the early days, is interesting. For one thing, she shares photos of herself before and after heading to yoga. These weren't especially glamorous photos, mind you, and the "after" photo was also marked by her hair being a bit frazzled and her skin coated in a fine glow of her efforts, but what I got from them (as did several commenters) was motivation to do my own fitness efforts each day, and that's why I thought it would be interesting to see her perspective on a day-in-the-life for using Google+.

Time Used per Day: 30–60 minutes (done in small spurts throughout the day)

Primary Goals of Usage: Convert to community, learning, build audience, and social interaction

Number of Original Posts per Day: 3–5

Number of Shared Posts per Day: 5+

Number of Comments per Day: Varies. 10+/post

Links to My Blog or Projects per Day: 1–2

Number of Off-Topic Posts per Day: 1–2 (of my own). Usually the posts I share by other people are the off-topic posts.

Typical Strategy: What's different for me on Google+ is that I purposely started off with no strategy and went with more of a "gut instinct" approach. My thinking was, I can write about health, nutrition, and fitness endlessly on Google+, like I do everywhere else, or I can do something different. So, I decided to start posting pictures of myself practicing what I preach. The pictures range from me not wanting to get out of bed in the morning, to being all sweaty after a yoga class, to pure silliness. What I've found is that people respond to them. Because I'm (visually) sharing my life, they can relate, they see that I walk the walk, they get inspired and I'm not being preachy by telling anyone what they should or shouldn't be doing. This has led to inquiries for my services and increased viewership on my show.

Notes: Up until Google+ came out, Twitter was where I spent most of my time. I'm on Facebook as well, but the platform never fully resonated with me, and so I mostly use it to keep in touch with family and friends. What I loved about Google+ right away was that there is so much room to play. I can write more than 140 characters; I can see actual posts and pictures without having to click a link; I can decide whom I want to share my posts with; and because people have the ability to add me to their circles, I am "meeting" tons of new people.

By showing her daily practice, Jacqueline reinforces her commitment to health and yoga. By using photos instead of tweets and blog posts, Jacqueline adds a personal connection element that gives her community a face to the actions, so to speak. This is something you could do for your business, even if you're a desk jockey. Showing your mug every day hard at work, especially if you can find a way to make it fun and varied, can give a connective benefit.

Some Partially Fictitious Day-in-the-Life-of Suggestions

I came up with some ideas for how other businesses and professionals can use Google+ for business by creating sample day-in-the-life-of experiences for different business professionals. I then went back and asked representatives from these industries what I got right, and what they'd do differently. This section includes what we came up with for you.

These started as fictionalized day-in-the-life-of bits, and then I found a real person, so the use of "I" is to make it easier to personalize. I don't personally represent all these professions.

The Author

Time Used per Day: 1 hour (broken into two 30-minute blocks)

Primary Goals of Usage: Research ideas, connect with readers

Number of Original Posts per Day: 2–3

Number of Shared Posts per Day: 4–5

Number of Comments per Day: 10–20 (a lot of back and forth with readers)

Links to My Blog or Projects per Day: 0 (I don't blog.)

Number of Off-Topic Posts per Day: 1–2 (As an author, everything can be on topic.)

Typical Strategy: I want to connect with my readers and let them feel like they're on the "inside" of my projects. This builds up anticipation, plus drums up sharing activities to potentially grow the initial purchase of the book. I also show Amazon and other online book preorder links.

Special Uses: I use Google+ for a lot of research. (And yes, sometimes "research" is a bit sketchy and far-fetched.)

Notes: Writing can be lonely. I admit to using Google+ as a water cooler from time to time, a place to get ideas and thoughts from outside sources, and to just feel "seen" during the loneliness of writing.

Takeaway: The more you can build excitement around your project and make people feel like it's theirs as well, the better your interactions.

The Real Estate Agent

Time Used per Day: 2 hours

Primary Goals of Usage: Post community news, share listings, and share photos

Number of Original Posts per Day: 5–7

Number of Shared Posts per Day: 8–12 (I share a lot of community news.)

Number of Comments per Day: 30+. Connecting is a huge part of selling homes and commercial property, so I'm on here constantly, meeting people who identify themselves as being from (or coming to) my area, and talking with those in the community.

Links to My Blog or Projects per Day: 3–5. I admit I use this heavily to promote my listings.

Number of Off-Topic Posts per Day: 2–3 (It's important to show my humanity.)

Typical Strategy: I want to be the connector in my community. For people to feel that, I stay on top of the local news, however big and small, and I share what's valuable.

Special Uses: By curating so much, I get a lot more value than creating my own posts. But because people feel like they "know" me by what I share, they comment a lot on my original posts, too.

Notes: I'm seeing a lot of value in Google+ as a real estate professional. I've created lots of video walkthroughs, and I've even hosted local Hangouts that I use as digital "meet and greets."

Takeaway: Being there between sales is the key to real estate professionals' use of social networks. By giving past customers, current prospects, and potential future customers some interesting "connective tissue" in between transactions, there are many opportunities for connections and referrals, which are two of the four best parts of social networks and social media.

The Reporter

Time Used per Day: 2–3 hours (Some days, I'm glued to Google+ and Twitter.)

Primary Goals of Usage: Source gathering, story building, and commenting

Number of Original Posts per Day: 1–3

Number of Shared Posts per Day: 12–15 (I share a lot!)

Number of Comments per Day: 10–15. Connecting in the comments matters.

Links to My Blog or Projects per Day: 1–2. I point people to my news articles and my video posts.

Number of Off-Topic Posts per Day: 0 (Is that bad?)

Typical Strategy: Be the source of news, or at least one of them. Show my human side, which is important, too.

Special Uses: Video Hangouts with prospective story sources. Team video Hangouts with my crew. I also use Huddle on my Android phone.

Notes: What matters most is to gather up elements for a story, so I do that a lot here. I find that having more sources helps, so I've circled people into categories such as Tech News and Boston, and Best Of (for my top-shelf commentators).

Takeaways: If I were a reporter using this service, I'd throw in a bit of off-topic conversation. Even a nightly newscast has the lighter news or the silly anecdote. I think some reporters and news professionals fear that adding their own voice to their stream impacts their sense of impartiality. Society has grown up. We know our reporters aren't robots. We know they have personalities. It's okay to share that on Google+.

The Sales Executive

Time Used per Day: 1 hour

Primary Goals of Usage: Networking and prospecting

Number of Original Posts per Day: 1–3

Number of Shared Posts per Day: 7–10

Number of Comments per Day: 50+. Comments are where I spend most of my time. I might not always make new stuff show up, but I search out great profiles and comment on them all the time.

Links to My Blog or Projects per Day: 0. I don't blog. But sometimes I link to things I'm selling or to people who need help. I'm a connector.

Number of Off-Topic Posts per Day: Everything I do is off topic. Or maybe it's more that what I post I consider an important topic. I connect with people.

Typical Strategy: Build relationships and keep them warm. Comment, comment, connect, comment, and connect....

Special Uses: I don't like Hangouts, but my sales team uses Huddle a lot. I stay active in the comments section, making sure that people know I find them interesting and making sure they connect to people who can help them. I'm at the elbow of every deal I can find on Google+, and as a longer-term effort, I think this pays off. The phone's suddenly ringing more often.

Notes: Not everyone has time to waste online all day. I'm never at my desk. But I do find myself sitting in waiting rooms while on sales calls ALL THE TIME, so when I'm there, I log into Google+ from my iPhone, and I post updates, and I live in the comments section. Sometimes, I share my location data, and other times, there's no way I want someone knowing I'm at their competitor's office. You must be smart about that.

Takeaway: That the sales professional doesn't like Hangouts makes sense. She has too much to do as it is, and sitting around on live video chats seems wasteful. The Huddle feature enables fast messaging back and forth, and that feels more reasonable for her time management. Remember, just because there are all kinds of features built into Google+, you don't need to use them.

The Educator

Time Used per Day: 3 hours (or more!)

Primary Goals of Usage: I'm running three courses online using Google+ as my collaboration platform.

Number of Original Posts per Day: 5–7

Number of Shared Posts per Day: 1–3 (if they relate to the courses)

Number of Comments per Day: 30+ (I answer a lot of questions.)

Links to My Blog or Projects per Day: 10–12 links to other sites and reference materials

Number of Off-Topic Posts per Day: 0, but only because I don't want to distract my students.

Typical Strategy: I use Google+ as a kind of digital classroom in between my in-person sessions. I use it to post links to homework assignments (everyone has a blog of some kind to post their longer assignments) and use it for the Hangout feature quite a lot. There are more than 10 students in my class, though, so that sometimes feels a bit exclusionary by nature. Recently, I decided to do it in shifts to alleviate that problem.

Special Uses: Lots of my students use Google+ to connect with current online leaders in the spaces we talk about. When we recently wanted to talk about green automobiles, we found representatives from Nissan, Toyota, and Tesla Motors to talk to us.

Notes: Before this, we used an expensive and frustrating piece of collaboration software. I'm not sure how that industry hopes to compete with FREE, now that Google+ solves a lot of issues for me.

Takeaway: The potential for Google+ is huge for educators. It's not built as specifically as some education software, but what the platform lacks in specific-for-educator tools, it makes up for by creating fast and simple connections between people with no-cost and browser-based tools.

The Photographer

Time Used per Day: 1 hour (sometimes more when I'm not as busy)

Primary Goals of Usage: Share photos, attend photography Hangouts, and meet and talk business bits with others

Number of Original Posts per Day: 20+ (if you count photo sharing)

Number of Shared Posts per Day: 10–15 (I share other great photos that I find.)

Number of Comments per Day: 5–10 (For whatever reason, I don't comment as much as I should, but I press the +1 often.)

Links to My Blog or Projects per Day: 3–5 (I share links to my main site with every grouping of photos I post.)

Number of Off-Topic Posts per Day: 3–5 (That's the nature of the business. We talk about whatever interests us.)

Typical Strategy: Nothing major. I just like sharing my best work. The critiques I get back often help me grow or inspire me to try something different. It's changing how I see my craft.

Special Uses: Naturally, I use the photo-sharing feature the most, but friends have shown me ways to make slideshows with music and upload them to YouTube, so I've started doing that, too.

Notes: I could probably get more out of Google+ than what I'm getting, but I think that the more I share, the more it's improving my work, so I'm not going to knock it. I like it more than Twitter and Facebook because I can see something immediately versus clicking a link on Twitter, and because it's a bit more open than Facebook. I don't use Flickr as much any more, except to post my photos. (Meaning, I don't comment as much there.) I feel like photographers are coming over to Google+ for more sharing and presentation.

Takeaway: Photographers are already using the site en masse. The sharing capabilities are giving people a nice way to present their work. I think where it will pick up is when photographers can set up business pages and invite people to engage and book new business.

The Business Executive

Time Used per Day: 30 minutes

Primary Goals of Usage: Reading, keeping up

Number of Original Posts per Day: 1 (if that)

Number of Shared Posts per Day: 7–10

Number of Comments per Day: 1–2 (I don't comment much.)

Links to My Blog or Projects per Day: 0 (I don't blog.)

Number of Off-Topic Posts per Day: 0

Typical Strategy: I use Google+ to keep up on interesting news and interesting people. I still use Twitter for this as well, and Google Reader, but I like the interface on Google+, and I'm getting a lot from my half hour of reading various links. I never EVER read the main stream or Incoming. It's too unfiltered. I have a few trusted sources that don't share animated gifs and cat photos, and I prefer their posts.

Special Uses: I'm using Google+ as an information hub and it's suiting my needs quite fine. It hasn't replaced anything (maybe someday, I'll stop using Facebook), but it gives me a different view than what Twitter alone gives me.

Notes: One of my social media managers complained that I don't post original content and that I'm not "joining the conversation." I don't want to join the conversation. I'm using it like a news reader. There is nothing wrong with this usage.

Takeaway: This executive is saying that she reads Google+ like a news feed. Depending on how she sets up her circles, this might give her targeted news that pertains to her business. Twitter can be used this way, as well, but the richness of what people can share gives her more interest in using Google+ at present.

Wrapping Up

This chapter looked at how others use Google+ for their own business pursuits and interests. You've read reports from busy executives of leading technology companies to authors, to fitness professionals, and many more. Including some of my "fictitious" efforts at the end, there are serving suggestions galore for you to start considering in building your own usage of Google+.

Chapter 5, "First Moves with Google+," talks about the first moves you can make with Google+. This is a how-to chapter that gives you ideas about implementing some of what you've read about here and a lot of the nitty-gritty details for setting up and using Google+ for your needs.

4

Profiles and Examples of Google+ Business Users

In this chapter, I share some examples of people who use Google+ in an interesting way. Most companies use Google+ business pages to simply post a link to their websites or blog posts, but some companies use Google+ in a creative way to promote their businesses.

Please note that in all cases except for Mike Elgan, I sought no personal insight from the people mentioned in this chapter—these are just my observations of their efforts. Because Mike Elgan receives great attention and awareness for his efforts, I decided to ask him a few questions.

Mike Elgan—Media Maker

Let's start with the power user of Google+, Mike Elgan. Mike is a media maker who writes for magazines and online sites such as *Cult of Mac, PC World, The San Francisco Chronicle*, and many more. At the time of this writing, Mike has 1.2 million (MILLION!) people who follow him on Google+. Why do so many people follow Mike? Well, he creates fascinating and varied media about topics that appeal to the first-level adopters of Google+. Mike is also an unofficial greeter and sharer of interesting people via his circle *"The League of Extraordinary Circle Friends."*

Who's in this list? Dan Ariely (who wrote *Predictably Irrational*), Esther Schindler (a technical editor of renown), Mignon Fogarty (Grammar Girl to you, bub!), Danielle Tunstall (artist of scary things), and, even me. At the time of this writing, Mike has inducted 35 people into this list, and he says that he wants to keep the list posted until at least 100,000 agree that they're extraordinary, too (only 3,000 to go before Mike will have to pull me from the list).

I communicated with Mike via Google+ (sent him a message), and he responded quickly. Being responsive on any platform is key to getting much use and value out of it, and this is no exception. Mike shared with me his favorite features of Google+ and why he uses it in the following:

- **Extreme flexibility**—"I use Google+ as a blog, primarily, and it's an easy blog to use and more 'social' than any other blogging platform, including Tumblr. The flexibility of Google+ enables me to also use it as I would a chat service, a microblogging service, and even as a substitute for a lot of email. I also use it as a photo gallery for sharing pictures with others and storing pictures for myself. My email newsletter is automatically created out of my Google+ feed, so that's another task I don't have to think about. I also auto-post from Google+ to Twitter and Facebook. The fact that I can do everything in one place means I don't have to do everything all over the place."

- **Conversations**—"There's no question that Google+ is the best place online for comment conversations. Blocking, deleting, and reporting tools give me powerful control to weed out anyone who would wreck those conversations. And an online comments conversation can easily evolve into a chat conversation or even video chat via Hangouts."

- **Social sharing and SEO**—"The combination of social sharing and SEO for public posts is magic. People used to talk about blogging as being out on the open web and about social networking posts being locked away in dead-end cul-de-sacs. But now the opposite is true. A blog can be the dead end, with posts just sitting there without being discovered.

A post on Google+, however, can be shared and reshared, introducing itself to new eyeballs serendipitously. And everything that happens on Google+ is thoroughly and instantly indexed for discovery through search and available to the public, even if they don't have a Google+ account. Google+ offers the most public and most discoverable channel for blog posts ever created."

Keep in mind that Mike is a media maker and his goal is to capture attention for his articles, networking to gather stories and relationships, and a general need for his materials to be found through a search. He doesn't sell advertising, so it's okay for him to use Google+ as a blog site—he's not losing money by diverting people to this platform. (I'd do that piece differently, but mainly because I consider Google+ an outpost and not a home base.) I learned the following from Mike regarding Google+:

- **Post 3–5 times a day**—Of these posts, consider a mix of personal news, pop culture news, helpful how-to information, and topics for extended discussion. This blend seems to be an Elgan-signature style and anyone would benefit to follow this method.

- **Comment for 20 or more minutes a day**—Mike is a voracious commenter, on his own posts in response to other people (which shows engagement) and also on other people's posts (which shows interest in other people's work, while subtly reminding people to check out what he's talking about).

- **Appeal to curiosity**—Mike finds a crazy mix of posts, from discussing bacteria found in beer to his popular "mystery pic," where he posts something interesting and engages the audience to decide what it is.

- **Self-promote (a little)**—It's better if you can make it self-effacing or otherwise poke fun at yourself.

Take these lessons and run with them. Remember that Mike's goal is attention for attention's sake with a side order of engagement, so consider how you would use Google+ for your business.

Matt Dooley—Intercontinental Hotels

Matt Dooley is a marketing professional for a chain of hotels. You can imagine that his Google+ page consists of hotel room photos. Actually, his page is dedicated to his own passions and interests. For example, Matt is a musician, so he posts music videos, such as live performances. He also posts interesting photos, Dr. Seuss bits, and facts about science and physics.

The least interesting thing Matt could do is tell us about his hotels in every post. Instead, you end up following someone like Matt because you are interested in the material he's passionate about in his personal life. You remember to check in with Matt when you find yourself thinking, "Who do I know in the hotel business?"

I suggest posting an *occasional* work-related post to keep up search rankings and to keep people reminded about what you do. Matt does an amazing job of staying interesting enough to earn a spot in one's circles, and that is enough for him to get the business when he's ready to ask for it. Does this make sense? If you like Matt's style, check out Terry Doner from TD Bank Group. It's worth following him if you like nature, photography, and eclectic interests.

Deepak Chopra—Spiritual Advisor

I'm a fan of Deepak Chopra's books, but I'm also interested in how he uses media. Google+ is a way for him to share a mix of pointers to his own projects and interactive experiences such as the following:

- Posts of the 2012 U.S. presidential election
- Links to his new YouTube channel, where he posts daily videos
- Links to his blog and a Q&A about a specific topic
- Photos of himself in California
- Pointers to current political stories
- Promotions of his children and their projects

Although Deepak doesn't have a lot of traction on Google+ (there aren't a lot of comments inside the platform), he has many comments on his primary blogs and sites where he posts the articles—perhaps that's valuable enough. At the time of this writing, he has over 400,000 people following him on Google+ and that number is climbing rapidly.

Deepak uses Google+ to guide people from the outpost (G+) towards his home base (his own website), which is a primary content and engagement strategy and one I recommend in almost all cases to businesses and professionals. This is probably the biggest lesson he can teach. Copy Deepak's style by posting a picture, daily or every other day, of yourself or something else that might engage your audience. Because he is a person of fascination and curiosity to his readership, the self-portraits are interesting. It helps you center your views of Deepak, the spiritual solutions expert and the man living this life.

Rick Bakas—Wine Personality

I've known Rick Bakas for a few years, and have even had him speak at an event of mine. Rick wears a few hats, including marketing for a company, but he lists himself as a "wine personality" on Google+, making Rick one of two people when I think about wine.

If you look at Rick's Google+ page, prepare to have your stomach start growling. Rick often shows gorgeous photos of food that he has paired with various wines. I'm looking at a grilled ribeye in a port reduction sauce right now, and even though it's past midnight and even though I had a bowl of ice cream a few hours ago as a dessert, I'm thinking about red meat now. Thanks, Rick! When using Google+, you can learn the following from Rick:

- **Use photos to their fullest**—Rick doesn't just point and shoot: he thinks about his shot, makes sure it looks amazing, and posts great pictures to whet your appetite.

- **Stick to your theme and extend it**—On Mother's Day, Rick posted a photo of his mom and him tasting wines together. It came with a location tag, so that we can find the winery mentioned.

- **Share others in the industry's posts**—This is my *favorite* move out of all business moves in social media. Rick does not view other people who post about wines to be "competitors." Rick shares posts from others in his space, thus promoting passion overall and not just his own agenda.

- **Share the recipes**—Rick's passion for food obviously pairs well with his wine, and he's willing to share recipes; for example, he demonstrates one method of making ribs.

- **Go off-topic**—Although Rick posts sparingly when it comes to off-topic matters, you can learn something else that might draw you into liking him more. This is a golden opportunity for anyone.

Bill Gross—Serial Entrepreneur

So, what do you do with your Google+ page if you have several business pursuits? If you are the amazing Bill Gross, you just cover all your passions in one place and hope that the eclectic nature serves you well. That's what I see from the outside looking in, at least. Here's a sampling of Bill's posts:

- An infographic of the distribution of birthdays and a question that sparked a discussion on the math of it all.

- A photo of a steak cut to look like a map of the U.S.A. that also promotes one of Bill's investments, Chime.in—Bill takes every opportunity to focus on his company.

- Fascinating photos, funny photos, and thought-provoking photos—Bill nurtures the relationships coming from comments, which is something valuable to an investor and entrepreneur like Bill.

- A charity auction.

- Posts about financial indicators.

Bill doesn't disappoint. He's certainly worth keeping in your circle, if you want to think about trends, interesting posts, the future of industries, and new ideas. The main lesson I take from Bill is that there's room for a mix of ideas. It is difficult to qualify his posts into any particular theme, but that makes perfect sense if you're a serial entrepreneur. Bill's page becomes a way for me (and imagine I'm the CEO of a tiny startup or maybe the acquisitions guy from a big company) to see what catches Bill's eye, what he's interested in, and where he synthesizes his ideas. It's like mind-reading and learning what to do with a page like Bill's Google+ is also a lesson in learning how to share your interests and let potential partners, customers, or otherwise find out about you.

Jeremiah Owyang—Analyst, Altimeter

I've known Jeremiah for many years now. My first exposure to him was when I was somewhat critical of a white paper or a report of some kind (time has passed) that he released with a co-author, and I admit that I wasn't polite. What won me instantly to being a fan of Jeremiah's is that it didn't bother him that I was rude. Instead, he tried to educate me on his position, whether or not I chose to agree with it. I've admired him ever since.

As an analyst for a company that helps others with their business efforts, Jeremiah uses Google+ to ask questions so that he can start discussions to further his knowledge. On his page, it is common to find no fewer than six posts in a row with questions. I don't always know whether he asks questions out of curiosity or whether he's doing research for a client because of the variety of posts (for example, steak sauce preferences). His level of questioning and curiosity all fit his personality, and so people are willing to share what they feel or know with him. Here's what you can learn from Jeremiah:

- **Post plenty of questions**—To keep a particular discussion alive, follow up as often as people reply in the comments section.

- **Use Google+ as a scratch pad**—Jeremiah often writes small "pre-posts" on Google+ and then takes the results of the comments section into account when writing his final document, blog post, or article.

- **Share your travel pictures**—Jeremiah's business requires him to travel, so he gets to see and experience several interesting moments. He shares many of these on Google+, which keeps people interested in him and not just his work.

Jeremiah makes it known that he's a thoughtful and professional analyst, while still letting his personality shine through. This is one of many reasons why he gets businesses to take notice of his work and that of Altimeter. His Google+ presence is also something that serves his company and his clients well, while not feeling like an agency presence.

What About a Brand Page Doing Something Interesting?

When I surveyed the 150 brand pages I follow, everyone from Red Bull (the beverage company) to Sony to the *Economist*, most posts were pointers to blogs or entertaining quizzes. For the most part, brand pages consist of people and companies still wondering where Google+ fits into their larger social business efforts. Take the advice of current Google+ users, such as those in this chapter, and apply it to your business page.

5

First Moves with Google+

You've signed up for Google+. Now what? In some cases, you've purchased this book because someone in the organization or a colleague told you, "You've really got to get on this Google+ thing, and you've got to start now, before everyone's here!" And some part of you said, "YES! That's exactly what I'll do! I'll sign up, get in there, and then I'll... I'll...."

Yeah, that happens. Don't worry about it. Hopefully, Chapter 3, "A Day in the Life," gave you some ideas by walking you through some of the day-in-the-life scenarios. Now, you want to dig in and start implementing some of what you've learned up until now. This chapter covers the steps and ideas of implementation at a higher level (with great detail here about your profile page and your privacy settings) and then Chapters 6, 7, and 8 discuss some more detail.

Consider profiles first, and then you can get into the other first moves.

Profiles Matter for Business

Profiles might make or break most people's immediate experience with Google+. Why? Because the profile is the first signal you have when connecting with someone. It's the first chance to make an impression. It's a lot like a business card blended with a peek at someone sitting in a waiting room. Because of that, it's important.

Using Your Google+ Profile for Business

In the early days of Google+, users were concerned with how they could best represent their businesses on the service. The first attempt at business pages was made by users simply changing the name on the account to whatever company they wanted to represent, and making their logo stand for their screen name.

But Google wasn't ready for this, and so it requested that companies take those accounts offline for a while, until it was ready to unveil its true intentions for business profiles. Some people were up in arms about it. Others felt like Google didn't understand how people would want to use this platform for business.

Here's another take: People could most certainly use Google+ for business long before Google was ready to release "official" business pages, even without violating any terms of service. People keep confusing the technology of "Google+ business pages" with what a business person does: connects with potential buyers and existing customers, and builds relationships that add value to both parties. Business pages are a great additional piece of technology to have, but by simply being on Google+ as a person representing your business, there's much to do.

Businesses Are Made of People

Chapter 3 includes some interviews with people actively using Google+ as representatives of business. In most cases, people are highlighted who represent larger companies, but a few small business owners are included as well.

Jennifer Cisney is Chief Blogger for Kodak, but she also represents herself on Google+. When she shares interesting posts about photography and video, we *know* she's sharing something that Kodak will approve of as part of her role, but it also comes off as authentically sharing her interest in the subject matter of the films or photos.

Scott Monty is the head of social media for Ford, and as such, his stream has a lot of content about Detroit and surrounding cities (he lives there) and also talks about the automotive industry. However, just as with Jenny Cisney, there's a lot of Scott in there, and these personalities matter.

Darren Rowse of Problogger *is* his business. When people connect to his stream on Google+, they see pictures of his family that give you a sense of him but that also promote his Digital Photography School. When you look at what he's sharing, there's a natural inclination to want to get involved in his business.

In all cases, these people are representative of their business. They are not the "official Kodak page" or the "official Ford page" or the "Problogger" page. These people represent a business that you can get to know, and that can lead us to helpful information that can improve your world. Businesses are made of people—you don't need to talk to Ford. You can talk to Scott.

Connections Before the Sale

Google+ is a platform that can enable people to connect to people, and you, as a representative of a business, have some steps to take to build those relationships. One of the most important parts to get your best business value out of using Google+ comes from getting your profile put together, and building the other human elements that people will respond to upon seeing it.

If you look up Chris Zoller from PolarUSA (maker of fitness accessories and the like), his bio reads as follows:

> "Customer experience thinker, community manager, content creator, father, triathlete. I like creating amazing consumer experiences by combining today's tech with good old-fashioned local hardware store love."

This is the kind of person you'd want to do business with. You might think, "Huh, maybe I should check out what Polar sells, because I'm sure Chris wouldn't work for a company full of jerks." Wouldn't you want that kind of reaction for your business?

Chris is sharing stories and information of interest to the fitness community. If you're interested in this, you can see something of interest through what Chris shares. But when you go to his profile and see his language, about hoping to give his community "good old-fashioned local hardware store love," you have a strong sense of what kind of person Chris is, and by extension, you share those feelings with the brand Chris represents: Polar.

Mike Bowler is in the real estate business. He does training, consulting, and selling. When you visit his stream, you can find a mix of local Michigan interest items (which lets you know that he cares about his community and it gives you interesting items from the area he services), stories from the real estate community at large, praise to his colleagues and community members, videos from Mike about what interests him, and more. The humanity of Mike shines through and says to you, if you're in the market to buy or sell a property in Michigan or if you want to train your team of real estate professionals, that Mike is the man for you. Business is made up of people.

If you're Richard Binhammer at Dell, you're part of a larger corporation, and you have a somewhat more defined role. It's a lot easier to be personal and personable, and yet the company requires that Richard shows results that justify his time on various social networks such as Google+. To that end, Richard almost has it easier than if you represent a small business.

If you are president of a small design firm, you have a lot more of the burden to represent the company. And yet, if you don't balance your personal self with your business self, you'll miss the opportunity to build relationships before the sale.

Now let's start on profiles, and then work from there.

How You Appear to Others

Often when established users of Google+ come across someone new (such as your-self, perhaps), the first view they have is of Figure 5-1.

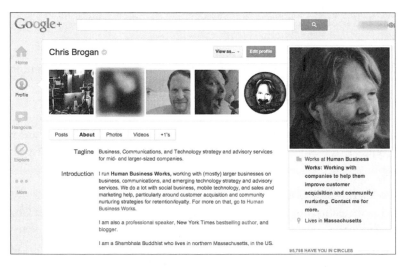

Figure 5-1   Brief user information in Google+.

Now, when people see this, they can decide a few things. "Hmmm, I've never heard of Chris, nor have I heard of Human Business Works, so maybe I won't circle him." Or they might think, "Well, he runs a company of some kind, so maybe that means something to me." But because they see that information, they have just a little bit more to go on before deciding in a split second whether they want to add you back to a circle of their choosing.

This is just the first part of the importance of making sure your profile is in good working order. There are more steps, but initially people make choices.

Other things to consider, obviously, while looking at the previous picture and text is whether your avatar profile is helpful to people deciding whether to add you to one of their circles. If you have a cute, fluffy kitty, it's less likely that you represent some business of significance to the people viewing you—unless you're fortunate enough to be in the cute, fluffy kitty business.

That preview of your profile is people's first view of you—their first inkling into whether they should consider connecting with you. That's a great reason to give it some attention.

Danie Ware's profile is succinct but gives you a sense that she's creative, artistic, multi-faceted, and definitely not your typical person to connect with (see Figure 5-2). The beauty in this is that when you stand out in the crowd, you get more opportunity. Danie's clearly a "Plate-Spinner Extraordinaire."

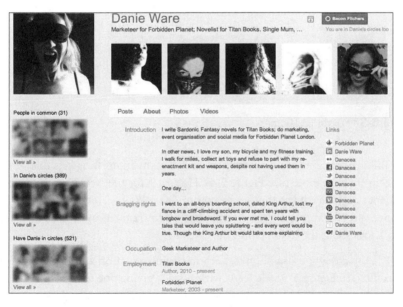

Figure 5-2   Danie Ware. Courtesy of Danie Ware, http://danieware.com.

David B. Thomas used to work with me, and we've known each other for a few years now. He gives you insight into what matters most by leading with being a dad and husband (see Figure 5-3). In his business section, he starts with his new book with links right to where one can purchase it. And then Dave finishes with his work history and a link to his professional site. What I like is that his profile is well rounded.

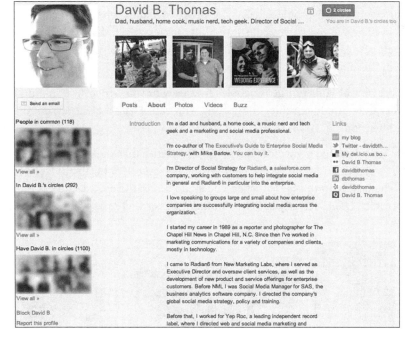

Figure 5-3   David B. Thomas.

Nick Bilton's profile is brief, but in there are so many interesting bits that one simply needs to learn more (see Figure 5-4). He writes for the *New York Times*, but that's not nearly as cool as the fact he cofounded NYCResistor and that he's "jumped out of 50 perfectly good airplanes." I admire the brevity, plus the ability to get to know about the man behind the column.

Rick Klau makes good use of links, both in his introduction and in the sidebar of his profile (see Figure 5-5). He leads with his CV, giving one the sense of his capabilities, plus a hint of what you could do with him professionally. Rick also uses the "scrapbook" photos above his profile to good effect, leading you in to want to learn more.

Scott McCloud's scrapbook photos to the right of his profile are the best part (see Figure 5-6). His clever use of an eye plus time equals a comic's progression is the perfect shorthand for his most well-known work, the book *Understanding Comics*. Scott's also done a lot to use appropriate anchor text (the text that shows up in blue

Figure 5-4   Nick Bilton.

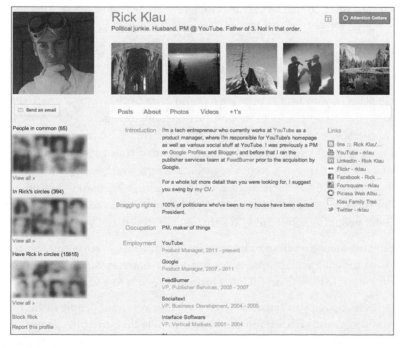

Figure 5-5   Rick Klau.

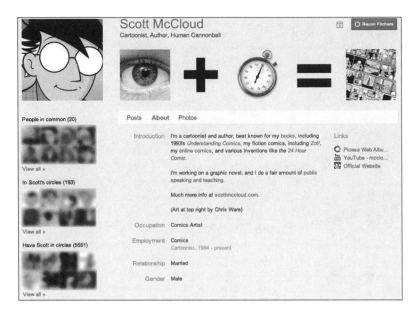

Figure 5-6   Scott McCloud. (Top right graphic copyright Chris Ware.)

to indicate a link), so that he can use Google+ to try to boost his ranking for the terms "online comics" and "public speaking and teaching."

Your About Page: The Basics

The elements of your profile page are a photo avatar, your name, a small "summary line" below your name, a spot for your introduction, "bragging rights," your occupation, your employment, your education, places where you've lived, relationship status, a sense of what you're looking for, your birthday, your gender, other names (in case of a maiden name or a common spelling error), a nickname, and whether your information should be visible in a search (see Figure 5-7). Besides this, in the right column, there is a spot for links, where you can insert links to other social networks plus point people to important URLs that matter to you and your business.

You can also choose whether to let people send you email via your profile page. They can't see your actual Gmail account address, but they can click a button (if you expose it) that lets them fill out a form and send it to you.

Via this About page, you can also control whether you want people to view who you've added to your circles. You can choose to hide that, and then people see only who has added you to their circles via your About page. (I'm not sure of the value to show or hide that data, but I currently have mine hidden, so as not to upset or offend anyone that I haven't chosen to add to a circle yet.)

Figure 5-7   My profile page.

The other tabs on your profile include the following:

- Posts, which shows what you've posted

- Photos, which shows people photos that you've uploaded where you and others have been tagged in the same photo, and photos that others have chosen to share of you

- Videos, which shows videos that you've uploaded to Google+ (and not your YouTube account specifically)

- +1s that you've shared via the +1 function OFFSITE (versus the +1s you give things on Google+)

Start at the Top

This feels like a lot of stuff to cover. When you get to your About page, click the Edit Profile button in the upper right, and now, when you hover over various sections of the page, you see that you can click them to edit them.

For instance, if you click the little blue Change Photo link below your profile photo (or avatar, as it is often called), the system enables you to upload a photo or pick one from your existing albums, pictures people have posted of you, mobile uploads, and so on.

Your Profile Photo

Your profile photo tells people a lot about you. If you choose something too formal (those photos that look like they're the grown-up equivalent of a school photo, complete with a cloud-like background), people will get one sort of impression.

The opposite can happen when you choose a red-eyed (from flash) snap of you where someone else was in the photo, but you've cut them out because it was a good smile. That never comes off as especially professional or inviting, either. There's a kind of happy medium you should aim for in these matters.

Shoot for something personable that might also give a sense about who you are outside of work, if that's acceptable and of value. For instance, perhaps you're not only the vice president of your bank, but maybe you're an avid fly-fishing enthusiast as well. This would make for a great avatar photo, insofar as it gives another view of you and humanizes you to your audience.

Following are some tips about how to choose avatar photos:

- Don't include photos of your kids as an avatar. People friend you, not your children (or pets).

- Photos of your company logo are far less engaging than photos of you.

- Cartoonized avatars are only cool if you're an illustrator or someone in a business that relates to these.

- Check whether you think your photo qualifies for "also looks a bit like a serial killer." (Some people choose "interesting" photos to represent themselves on the web.)

Editing Your Name

The Google+ profile editor enables you to edit your name as it appears in Google+. You might be inclined to add something to your name that you want people to think about when they see you. But if you change your profile name here, by clicking your name and then typing in something new, you might run into a problem.

If you edit your name on the Google+ Profile page, it changes that information on all other Google accounts related to this one. Meaning, if you change your Google+ profile name to "Dave 'The Incredible Plumber' Taylor," it's going to change your Gmail account and your Google Calendar account, and everything else that's tied to it. So, in short, you might not want to do that.

Editing Your Tagline

Think of the line below your name on your profile page as a summary line or a place for a tagline. What it might *best* serve as for you would be the answer to the sentence, "What do you do for your prospective customers?"

At the time of this writing, I have a little comment about what I believe I do for the world, plus I put an immediate and obvious link to my primary website URL. By the time this book is printed, I will probably have edited it some, and that's okay. To me, this little piece of territory might be best used flexibly.

Your little "summary" section might be something you change often, like an announcement, for instance, or a status. Maybe not, but it's an idea. For instance, if people hovered over your summary in the fall, they could be sent to a blog post or an article on your primary site that talks about how your business works in this season. The idea, simply, is that you can have some fun with this summary because it's visible only when someone clicks your About tab on your profile, and as such, it means they're open to learning more about you.

The Most Important Part of Your Profile: The Introduction

At this point, maybe you're thinking, "Geez, Chris. We get it. You want the profile to be robust and good." But to me, there's a lot to consider, especially because every time I survey other people's profiles, I'm left with an urge to shake many of these people and say, "You could be doing *so much more business*, if only you'd consider a few updates and improvements to how you use your profile page. So, that's why I hammer this home.

In your introduction, write it so that people understand how you might work with them. Blend this with some personal information so that people understand what matters to you outside of business. Be sure to use links inside that text; although be wary of having too many links. (Because too many links leads to the opposite effect of what you want: People won't click anything.)

My own profile is about as messy as my business life. I work for a lot of projects and companies. Therefore, I've done my best to explain how I work for large companies in one capacity, and how I work for smaller companies in another capacity.

In your case, try to be clear about how others will work with you. Explain what services or offerings you present. Be clear about what you do for your organization. Don't write a novel, but give it more than a sentence. For instance, maybe you can say this:

> "I teach franchise owners how to empower their franchisees, and I help franchisees navigate the complex waters of running a franchise. I consult in person and via online courses. If you want to see a sample of my online courses and some testimonials from professionals I've helped, click here."

That would simply sum up what you're doing and give people a sense of what they can do with you. That's the goal. Try to hook someone in the grand theater of no attention span.

A LITTLE TRICK ABOUT YOUR INTRODUCTION AREA

If you want to finish your Introduction section in style, do this: Put a way to contact you at the bottom of the introduction. That way, when people decide you're interesting and might be useful to their business needs, they know how to reach you. Do NOT include a link to your website but include a link directly to how people can contact you, or an email address and a phone number. I put a link to my primary contact form so that people can reach me easily.

Employment: A Useful Hack for You

When you fill out the Employment part of your profile, the part of your employment that's "current" is what shows up when someone hovers over your name in a post or in a comment. *That* is where you can insert a useful summary of what you do to catch people's attention.

Mine, at the time of this writing says this:

> Human Business Works: Large Business Digital Marketing Strategy & Advice and Small Business Tools and Smarts.

Write yours in a way that it engages people. It can be reasonably simple—actually, it's probably better that it is simple—but it must be engaging.

Instead of "Marketing Manager for Pearson Publishing," consider writing something such as "Finding great books about education and sharing them with people who love books." See how that might lead to more engaging interactions?

Create yours accordingly.

The Links Section

The Links section of your profile is probably the second most important part after the Introduction because it's where people can learn more about you and where you can point people to the specific pages or sites that best extend your conversation.

This is another situation in which a little goes a long way. Consider not sharing every potential place where people can connect with you. Consider also pointing people toward specific pages or posts on your sites, instead of to the main link, unless the main site URL is the best representation of continuing the conversation.

For instance, if you have a page that talks about your services, point people to that. Remember that you can select what text you want the link to present, so maybe a photographer's will say "Photography for Corporate Projects." It's up to you how you use it.

Moving on from the Profile

The profile can improve your potential chances to build business relationships on Google+. You can do this in many ways, but hopefully what this chapter covers gives you enough to start. If you have questions, you can always connect with me via Google+ and ask specifics: http://gplus.to/chrisbrogan.

6

Circles

The best part of Google+ is Circles, which is how the platform enables you to organize the people you choose to follow and connect with. It's also probably the part of Google+ that most people skip or don't do much with, and then wish they could go back and do it all over again. The good news is that you can go back and do it again. But maybe, if we do some things together, you won't have to do that. Figure 6-1 shows you what my main Circles page looks like.

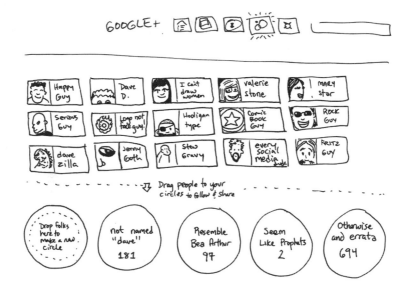

Figure 6-1   The main Circles page.

What Circling Means

As shown in Figure 6-1, Google+ enables you to organize the people you choose to follow by adding them to circles. This means that you have opted to receive any public posts they've shared, plus, if they choose to follow you back and add you to one of *their* circles, you can see whatever posts they share with your circle.

Now walk through that a moment. If you circle me, for instance, that means you've opted to receive anything I post to the public. If I don't circle you, and then I choose to post something to *only* my circles, you won't see it. If I've circled you under Good People, and I share something only with Attention Getters, you won't see that post, either.

Conversely, just because you've circled someone, it doesn't mean they'll see your posts, even if you mention them in a post. (Chapter 7, "Posting in the Stream," talks about what that means.) The act of circling someone simply means that you've chosen to add them to people you follow. It doesn't mean you've opened two-way communications between them.

How Do I Know Who Is Circling Me Back?

You can look for who is circling you in three ways. First, if you're looking at someone specific, you can just click that person's name, and you get to his profile page.

Under the big red button that says Add to Circles, it'll say something such as You Are in Vincenzo's Circles.

You can also look by going to https://plus.google.com/notifications/circle (see Figure 6-2).

Figure 6-2   Notifications of people who have added you to a circle.

This enables you to see who's added you to a circle lately, and it's a handy place to decide whether you want to add them back.

Of the methods, this is the most visual way to see who has added you, but it's also probably the slowest method if you want to better understand who's who and whether you want to add them back. It's up to you how you want to organize people, but for me, it's option 2 for understanding who's added me and determining whether it's valuable.

The third way is to go to your main Circles tab (the fourth tab at the top of the Google+ page), and click People Who've Added You. On that view, if you see a little circle in the bottom right of the user's rectangle, you've added them back. If you don't, you haven't.

Reciprocal Follows

A question I'm frequently asked is whether you should circle back everyone who's chosen to add you to their circles. On Twitter, I used to say yes, and that there was no reason why not to follow someone back on Twitter. But this is different because who you choose to circle impacts what you see when you look at the regular stream, and it impacts who sees what you choose to post, and so on.

It is *not* required that you reciprocate and follow back everyone who chooses to follow you. That's a personal preference, and you can decide whether that's useful to you. On Google+, different than Twitter, I've decided not to circle everyone back who adds me. The reason is that the more people I add, the harder it is to manage the stream of information I choose to consume. You'll come to your own opinions, and you'll likely change them a few times.

You can hover over anyone's picture in this view. You see a name and occasionally some information under the name. Do you remember all that fuss I made in Chapter 5, "First Moves with Google+," about this? Now, you can see why.

Although it's probably more useful to know who has connected with you, the majority of work you'll do in circles is the organization of the people you've chosen to follow. Let's talk about how to arrange circles, what to do with them, and a few little technical tidbits. We start with naming the circles because this is every bit as important (in some ways) as deciding where to gather people.

Creating Circles and Naming Them

Click your Circles tab, which is the fourth button on top of the Google+ screen. Those little blue circles down at the bottom of the screen come prenamed, but you can change any of them to be what you want them to be. I *highly* recommend that you make that your first order of business.

To create a new circle, should you need a few more than what you see below, go to the dotted-line circle at the bottom-left corner of the screen, hover your mouse over it, and click Create Circle. Easy cheesy.

But *what* you name them and *how* you use them is something that we explore here, so look at a few ways to think about that.

First, realize that your circle names are private to you. You can call a circle "Big Fat Jerks" and put me in it, and I would never know. I'll just know that you have me in *a* circle. I guess, before you start creating circles like that, with names such as "People I'd Probably Sleep With" or some such name, I recommend keeping them named something that wouldn't offend, on the off-chance someone would find out.

My circle names don't often have specific meaning. But who goes where matters to me. My circle names look something like Figure 6-3:

Following are the names of my circles and what they mean to me:

- **Close:** For people who are close enough to me that I'd let them babysit my kids.

- **Keepers:** For a select few dozen people that I wouldn't want to miss their every utterance.

- **Good People:** For people I've met in my travels who I like and want to check in with from time to time.

- **Attention Getters:** For the interesting "big names" (who also sometimes chat a lot).

- **Bacon Filchers:** For business professionals in larger companies. (There's absolutely no reason why I called this circle Bacon Filchers, but I did it to be funny, and I don't want to change it now.)

- **Journalists:** For a bunch of professional journalists in print, TV, and otherwise.

- **MKTG:** This is an "outbound" circle, which I'll explain more about in a bit.

Figure 6-3   Example of circles named by Chris Brogan.

I have a few others. The point for now is that you can name your circles however you want. Let's talk about some potential ways to organize circles, which suggests a few other naming conventions.

Outbound Circles and Inbound Circles

Users of Google+ coined circles *outbound* or *inbound*. It isn't how Google looks at circles. Some of us have created outbound circles, meaning we group some people into circles based on things we want to share with them, but maybe not with others. For instance, if I'm sharing something interesting about marketing, I share it with my MKTG circle but not necessarily with everyone.

Inbound circles are simply groups of people you've organized by what they tend to share or how you choose to view them. For instance, if you have a Boston circle, that's where you'd tend to put people who live in and around Boston or who talk about it a lot.

There's technically no such thing as outbound or inbound circles, but you and I can create them to better understand how we use circles.

Sharing Circles

It is possible to share circles you've created with others. From the Circles tab, click the circle you want to share. You'll now see "Edit/Delete/Share." Click Share. You can then decide whether to share this circle with public (everyone) or with specific circles of interest. For instance, you could share your Competitors circle with your Teammates circle. Sharing really amps up the opportunity to collaborate.

Ordering Circles

On the main Circles page, you can rearrange circles so that they are listed in the order you choose. For instance, if you want to put your Important circle at the top of your list of circles to explore and then Vendors circle next in line, you can do that. Just drag and arrange.

Some people choose to put their inbound circles at the top and their outbound circles at the bottom so that they are clear about which circles to include when sending information out, for instance. That's a matter of choice. The arrangement of the circles simply changes how they are presented to you on the Home page of Google+ located at http://plus.google.com.

For some businesses, *where* you are makes a difference. For instance, Joe Sorge sells hamburgers at AJ Bombers in Milwaukee, so it would benefit him to know about other people who identify as being in Milwaukee. But Google+ doesn't immediately make this easy to figure out.

Pause for a moment and go to http://findpeopleonplus.com. This is an unofficial third-party site that scrapes publicly visible data from Google+ and organizes it into interesting categories. This might help you find locals, at least if some of those people have identified their location for you.

Following are a few other ways to potentially organize your circles—the first of which we just explained in a use case:

- **Local:** If you're in Boston or Mumbai, include a circle for people who are local to your area. This helps with prospects for your business and can give you more local news to keep current on what happens in your area.

- **Thinkers:** No matter what you call it, there are people you'll want to follow who have ideas that are different than yours and who make you think. This kind of circle is where you go for inspiration.

- **Competitors:** I personally don't do a lot of competitive analysis for my business, but that's me. If you're from Apple, maybe this is Dell employees. If you're a photographer, maybe you name this Colleagues but secretly think of them as competitors. It's your decision.

- **News:** I have a Journalists circle so that I can read what they're doing, comment on what they're talking about, and get myself generally known. Although this is partially so that I can appreciate their work, it's also so that they might get to know me, and then think of me, should a story arise that I could help with. You can do this in other ways, having journalists get to know you, but that is covered later.

- **Potential Employees:** Think about that. If you want to hire people to run community development for your great new software platform, maybe this is a way to keep an eye on them.

- **Vendors:** A lot of web design and WordPress people follow me, and I'm often asked for people who do that kind of work. Putting together a circle of people who do something that pertains to your business might be useful. It's like keeping a little directory handy.

- **Personal Passion:** I have a circle of comic book artists, writers, and professionals in that industry. This has no direct business value to me. I just love comic books and have since I was 5 or 6. Feel free to make a circle about something you care about, even if this is your business account and even if the bosses might frown on it. Know why? Because it's out of these serendipitous connections that can bring you other connections. That was how I interviewed Greg Pak (a writer, currently doing interesting stuff for Marvel Comics, among others) for this book.

- **Prospects:** Okay, so adding people to this circle is difficult at present. People don't exactly line themselves up and say, "I'm really anxious to buy what you're selling." But if you do a little searching and a little thinking, you might start to find ways to add people to a circle like this. Just realize something important: Just because someone looks like your prospect doesn't mean they're all that interested in you selling something to them. Tread gently.

Who Should You Follow?

As stated before, you can check at http://findpeopleonplus.com to see if any particular occupation, locale, or some other identifying factor helps you determine whether someone is interesting to follow. You can also search on Google.com by adding site:plus.google.com to your search, and then adding in a search term that you think might prove useful in finding someone of interest. If, for instance, you want to find people talking about yoga, you can type the following into Google: site:plus.google.com yoga.

If that doesn't narrow it down enough, you can add more search terms, and you can use a -term type of search to filter even more. For instance, I used the word "Boston" after "yoga" and found people talking about yoga and having something to do with Boston. It's not perfect, but it's one way to find more potential people of interest.

Friendsurfing

In the early days of using Google+, one way I found interesting people to follow was that I friendsurfed. By this, I mean that I would find someone whom I followed or found interesting, and I would click into that person's profile. From there, I'd see who he or she had chosen to add to his or her circles, and I would sometimes add some of the same people.

For instance, I just went to Greg Pak's profile, and I looked at who he was following. I found Evie Nagy from *Rolling Stone* and decided to follow her. I also found Christopher Yost from Marvel Studios and Adam Koford from Disney Interactive. I don't know any of these people, but if Greg finds them interesting, I thought I would give them a try.

By doing this, you can often find interesting new people to connect with, and there might be even more connections after following someone's content and information that they've shared. To me, friendsurfing becomes a potential way to make new connections of value. I wouldn't exactly attempt to sell anyone anything simply because you've chosen to add someone to a circle, but making a preliminary relationship is certainly not effort lost.

Do I Know You?

Often, you discover that people have circled you, but you aren't sure who they are. An easy way to tell is to hover over the name of the person, and you can see who you have in common at the bottom of the box that displays. I find this useful when determining whether someone might actually know me, or whether they're following me because I fit a certain "set" of people they're following. In my case, if I see people in my corner of the industry, such as Seth Godin, Brian Clark, Guy Kawasaki, and Robert Scoble, I know that someone's collecting a certain group of voices. Seeing this means that the person might be a "collector" seeking to gather up "top marketer" voices or something of that nature. I don't often circle these people back because they don't often communicate as much as they just read and share.

Again, these are personal choices, but when you see who you might have in common with someone, you start to understand whether this is someone you might choose to follow. Now, let me tell you a bit of a "hack" about this. If you're in business and you want to connect with someone specific (potentially someone of influence) in an industry, it is useful to connect with other people connected to that influencer. Meaning, if you want to connect and win business with Michael Dell, it wouldn't hurt to have a handful of people in common with him already circling you.

How you go about using this tip is up to you. If you stretch too far outside of your circle of "known" people, it's not likely that this can work. That said, I thought I'd mention it because it can be useful.

Should You Circle Celebrities?

There are, believe it or not, quite a number of celebrities (and their publicists) on Google+. I've seen Taylor Swift, 50 Cent, William Shatner, and many more celebrities using Google+. To me, this is a personal preference. If you're interested in following celebrities, feel free to put together a circle of them. Will they ever be useful for your business? It's not as likely that you can make a meaningful connection with a celebrity via this medium, with a few exceptions.

Observe how certain celebrities use these tools, and you can "smell" rather quickly who's having their publicist post for them and who's doing their own work. Wil Wheaton, famous in the past for *Star Trek: The Next Generation*, but relevant for *so* much more than that, is a power user of this platform and is fun to follow. You are likely to have a conversation with him. Ditto for Alyssa Milano. Ditto for a few other celebrities. But these are often the exception to the rule, sadly.

If you hope to do business with celebrities, I can't yet recommend Google+ as a useful tool for this. Use it to stay up on their comings and goings, but you should seek another venue for connecting. At least that's been my experience. It's not that there's any specific negative to circling celebrities, but you'll probably get their publicist's news stream and no real interaction to speak of, in lots of cases.

More About Outbound Circles

I've talked a few times in this chapter about outbound circles. By this, I mean that you have the opportunity to group together people in a circle so that you can send them specific information, while not sending it out to others. For instance, I have a marketing circle, where, if I want to talk specifically about marketing, I can target a post to that circle, and none of the other people who choose to follow my posts will see it.

This can be useful in a few ways. If you want to group together company teams into circles, you can. Imagine making a "project team" circle, and putting the specific employees and contractors in that circle, and then advising them all to do the same. *Pow*—instant, reasonably private communications and sharing. (I say "reasonably" because I wouldn't yet trust Google+ with specific company proprietary data. It is a public site.)

You can also use outbound circles for personal interests, obviously. Maybe you're into fitness and nutrition and you want to share recipes with a group of people into similar things. Perhaps you're a car enthusiast and like to share photos and videos of cars. If you're not interested in sharing with the general public, by all means, this is the way to do it.

Circle Tricks

You can put people in more than one circle. Simply hover over their name with your mouse, and you can see where you've listed them; then decide if you want to move these people to another circle by unselecting the old and selecting the new, or if you want to add these people to more than one circle. Just select the new circle or circles you'd like to add them to, and make sure those boxes are checked, too.

I have a few friends I've put in Close because I want to share specific things with them. I have a few of these friends also placed into Marketing because they opted into receiving information that I share with people about marketing. I have a good friend in four circles and counting because our interests relate in matters of health, marketing, and Buddhism. Plus, she's in my Close circle. You can do the same with select friends, work colleagues, and customers, if it makes sense to you and your business.

Another trick: If you want to copy everyone (or most everyone) from one circle into another circle (maybe you're promoting people from Not Sure to Interesting), simply go to the Circles page, and then click the circle you specifically want to copy from. When it displays, click the View Circle In tab. Then, go to the upper-right part of the screen, click More Actions, and choose Select All. Then, click and hold the mouse button down and drag everyone into the new circle (below) that you want to move them into.

Want to do all but one person? Hold down Command (on a Mac) or Control (on a PC) and click the person you don't want to move to the new circle. Easy as that, you've moved all (but one) to where you want them to go.

Circles Aren't a One-Time Thing

Organizing and re-organizing your circles is an ongoing kind of thing. For example, I find that sometimes people I've chosen to follow because of where they are employed doesn't always work. One employee of a large retail chain was in a marathon to post as many potential reshares of other people's content as humanly possible, so his reshares constantly showed up on my screen. I removed him from the circle after a bit, and things went back to normal.

As mentioned at the beginning of the chapter, setting up circles wisely can save you a lot of time, but you need to make some adjustments along the way. Don't make managing your circles a "job." When you have the occasional 10 minutes, slip into your circles to decide if you need to further define them. For instance, I have a circle that's built just for larger name-brand companies. I might go back and make a Tech Companies circle and separate them out from all the other interesting companies I follow. An ounce of prevention keeps you from having to rebuild your circles too often, though.

Wrapping Up

We covered a lot of ground here. Think of this: Consider whether to have inbound and outbound circles; remember that adding someone to your circles doesn't mean they see what you've posted until they add you back; know that you don't have to circle back everyone who chooses to circle you; and remember that you'll have to touch your circles more than once.

In the next chapter, we talk about what to post, how to post, when to post, and more. It will all tie together as we go along. You'll see.

7

Posting in the Stream

After setting up your profile and deciding who to follow and how to organize your circles, what becomes the lion's share of what you do on Google+ is most likely a blend of reading other people's posts, sharing and commenting on those posts, and creating your own posts. Sure, you might also do your share of hangouts (live video chatting), but for the most part, consuming, connecting via comments, and then creating new content of interest are the bread and butter of what you'll do.

There are personal ways to post and business-minded ways to post. From the outset, you need to think about and create material from both perspectives because people who choose to follow you as a representative of your company also need to connect with the human side of you. People connect with people. Even if you represent Pepsi, and you want to be the "voice" of Pepsi, people want to know about you.

This chapter talks about various ways to post information, including sharing other people's posts and commenting on posts, but mostly how to create and build business value with your own creative information. Also covered is video, photos, text, links, and more, and this chapter discusses how each post might be best used to build relationships with your prospective buyers and the community at large. However, first, start with a position and perspective that makes a specific strategic point.

Google+ Isn't a Blog, and It's More Than Twitter

In the early days of Google+, some people immediately announced that they were scrapping their primary web presence and using Google+ as their main blog/communications platform. While I understood their perspective (more interaction with more people potentially visiting more often), I felt that it was a bad choice. To me, the difference between your primary website or blog and something like Google+ is the same as the difference between a home and a hotel room.

Even if you put down an oriental rug and bring in a few lamps and some Van Halen posters for the walls, if it's not your own home, it's still a hotel room. There might be more people visiting Google+ than your blog in the aggregate, but that doesn't mean they're sticking around, and it doesn't mean they're getting the same interaction on Google+ as they can get on your primary website or blog.

Building anything on another company's platform is giving it the equity and taking away a lot of your potential capabilities. Google+ doesn't enable you to choose themes. It doesn't enable you to embed other technologies (unless already integrated by Google). Google+ doesn't make it easy for you to convert people from being a visitor to a prospect (such as inviting people to opt into your email newsletter). You need to consider countless more reasons. Suffice to say that I'm opposed to the idea of throwing away your main website and living primarily on Google+.

I've taken this same strategy/perspective a bunch of times, but it bears repeating. If your main website or blog is your "home base," Google+ is an outpost. As such, it's a place to connect, communicate, listen, and interact with people. This is actually where you'll spend a lot of your time because people frequent the outposts much more often than they visit your home base.

Your main site is where your primary transactional wish occurs. For instance, if you're a car dealership, perhaps your goal is to encourage people to come in for a test drive. Most dealerships do this by attempting to convert the web browsing prospect into someone who calls a salesperson or who fills out a contact form.

By contrast, people on Google+ might not be looking for a car, and if you're Aaron Manley Smith, owner of Motorphilia, a virtual car dealership (and the guy who sold me my 2010 Chevy Camaro SS), you're listening and building relationships on Google+ so that, when the time comes, people will know how to contact you and how to visit Motorphilia and start a transaction.

The goal of your work on an outpost (like Google+) is to build a relationship and nurture your prospects and community. The goal of your work on your home base is to convert people to an action, be that a sale, a membership, or something else.

One last point about this: This means that the goal of a home base is far more static and specific, whereas the efforts of being on an outpost (which is what I'm calling Google+) are far more nuanced and require a lot more effort and interaction. This is how it's meant to be. My goal in explaining this in detail before talking about posting is so that you understand where this fits into your larger business efforts and strategies. Hopefully, we're in agreement.

Posting on Google+

To post on Google+ from the web, click the Home link (which is the little House tab with the three dots and lines below it). This displays a Stream view, and a box that displays the text Share What's New in light gray (see Figure 7-1). Click anywhere in the box, and you see what is shown in Figure 7-2.

Figure 7-1   The Google+ Stream view.

Figure 7-2   The Share What's New box.

Following are the elements you see:

- A place to type in text.
- Four icons that enable you to choose between posting a photo, a video, a link, or location data. Note: you can share location data *and* post a photo, video, and obviously text.
- Sharing options, which are listed under the main post box.
- The Share button, which is how you execute your post.

In Google+, you have the option to type in text, select one of those four icons, and then determine with whom you'd like to share your posts. After you post something, you have a few more options, including the following:

- Editing your post
- Deleting your post
- Linking to your post
- Reporting or removing specific comments, which is helpful if people spam your comments section
- Disabling comments
- Disabling reshare

It's a little odd that Disable Comments and Lock This Post aren't visible until after you post. If you post something to the stream, you must then rush and click either or both of those options quickly before someone decides to do either. Perhaps this will be fixed in future versions, because it seems a bit awkward in practice, but you'll get the hang of it, if either of those functions is important to you.

We'll get back to how we use those later, but I wanted to bring them up because they're part of the posting mechanism that doesn't show up until after you click Share.

The Sharing Options Under the Main Post Area

Below the area where you put your post information is the sharing options for each post. You have several options to how you choose to share this information. The first of these, the kind of wide-open option, is to share with Public. This means that anyone can see this post. (Most of what I share is to the Public group.)

You can choose to share with Your Circles, which means that anyone you put into a circle can see the post. You can also add Extended Circles, which means that you've not only shared that information with people in your circles, but also made it visible to other people who have those people in *their* circles. (If that's a bit confusing, it's okay—it makes sense after checking things out.)

You can share with one specific individual by typing @username or +username and then making sure you haven't added any other sharing options. This is as close as Google+ comes to a private message.

Similar to this last option, if you mention someone in a post with the + or @ method (such that their name shows up in blue with a + before it), then that person will receive access to that post, whether or not they're in the circle (or circles) you've chosen to share that information with.

For example, assume you have a circle called Chris Brogan Haters, and you use it to share all kinds of mean and nasty information about me (hey, people might!). If you type into your box a bunch of information about how I don't floss my teeth enough, but you just say, "Chris has bad flossing habits," your secret evil club is safe. However, if you put in "+Chris Brogan has really bad flossing habits," and my name shows up with a + and is blue, I'm going to have access to see that post, even if I'm not in your "Chris Brogan Haters" circle. Make sense?

Interestingly, you can also share a post with someone not on Google+ by including that person's email address in the sharing area below. Simply click Add More People, and start typing in the email address. When it's all typed in, press your Tab key, and *poof*: You've emailed someone a copy of the post you're about to share.

SHARING SOMETHING WITH A LIMITED AUDIENCE

When you share something with a limited audience, the people who have received that post can see any mutual connections you've shared it with, plus get a count of how many other people had access to see the post. So, if you share with your Managers circle, and that's 24 people, any colleague who has a mutual connection in common with you will show up when one clicks the "limited" explanation that shows up to the right of the date stamp on the post (see Figure 7-3).

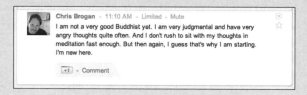

Figure 7-3   A limited post.

Formatting Posted Text

As noted, to post text, simply follow the preceding step of going to the Stream page (your little house) and clicking in the white area of the box that says, Share What's New. Type your text in and press Share.

You can also add bold, italic, and strikethrough text to format your text. Following are the methods for doing this:

- To bold text, put two asterisks (*) around the word or words you want to bold.

- To make your text italic, put two underscores around the word or words you want italic.

- To apply strikethrough to your text, place a dash (--) around the word or words you want to apply it to.

You can also post a link without having to do anything fancy. However, posting links into the text box makes the post become a "link" post; if you don't select something such as a photo, a video, or location data first. In other words, because a post can be *either* a photo post, a video post, or a link post, but not *more* than one of these types of posts, typing a link to a website into your "text" post turns it into a "link" post.

If you make a different type of post, such as a photo post, a video post, or a location data post, you *can* then add a link (or links) into the text part that accompanies that type of post. For example, if you post a photo, Google+ enables you to add text to that post. If you post a photo, and then mention that you took it in front of http://dell.com headquarters, that shows up as a link in the text part of that post, even though it's a photo post.

Likewise, you can add location data and not need to choose between types of posts.

Experiment a bit, and you'll get it.

Posting Photos

Photos are actually quite powerful in Google+. I've noticed (through testing) that if I post straight text, I get one level of reaction. If I post a photo and that same text, I'll get a lot more interaction. Why? I think it's just because we can use the photo to draw people into the story.

You choose three options to post a photo on Google+. You can simply add a photo, you can create a new album (or collection of photos), or you can post a photo from your phone (if you've taken photos and selected auto-post via the Google+ mobile app for Android or iPhone). Don't worry about the details of those last two options yet. Just think about posting a photo from the web app at first.

When you click Add Photos, the web application asks you to locate the photo you'd like to add. After you find and select that photo, Google+ uploads a copy of it and puts it on your post. Photos show up below the text you enter (should you choose to add text to the post) no matter what. So, you can't choose the location of where the photo is placed inside the post. It'll always be at the bottom (as will video, links, and placed data).

On the mobile application, you can set up Instant Upload as an option for photo sharing. This enables you to automatically upload photos (and videos, should you choose) to a private web album. You can do two things with this: Immediately select photos to post to your stream via the web application, or save the photos for later use when you decide to post via your web application (where the most recent photos that have auto-uploaded from your mobile device wait for you, should you decide to use them in a post).

Photos taken and uploaded via the Instant Upload don't immediately post into your stream. They simply go into a holding area until you choose to use them (if you want) for inclusion with a post. However, *posting* a photo via your mobile device does put that photo right into the stream, after you press share. Be aware of the difference.

Thus, if the boss says, "Take some photos of the event," simply taking photos and having them shoot up to Google+ via Instant Upload leaves them in a kind of limbo. So, you'll have to go in and *publish* those photos before they show in your stream. If you do it the other way around, and you're posting photos thinking that you're just lobbing them into Instant Upload to sort out later, and you include those photos of your boss drunk and falling out of the duck boat, that might not go well either. See the difference?

Posting Video

You can post video by uploading directly to Google+ via the web application, by posting something originally uploaded via your mobile device (see the above notes on how photos get sent to Google+ via mobile), and by pointing to a video already posted on YouTube.

Of these options, I've had the best success with posting via YouTube. When I've attempted to post directly from the web application, the quality of the video decreases, and the time it takes to upload is longer (even on my high-speed connection in the office). Instead, if you want to post a video of your own creation, it is probably easier to upload it to YouTube and then post it to Google+ by referencing the YouTube link.

If you're sharing videos from your own YouTube channel, and that channel is associated with the same Google account that you use for Google+, simply click the Video icon, select YouTube, and then select Your YouTube Videos from the next option.

Sharing other people's videos from YouTube is relatively easy. You can search for the video by name, or if you have the URL link specifically to that video, you can post into the appropriate spot after selecting Video, and then select YouTube. Either way, it usually comes right up. When you find what you want, select Add Video; then you'll be dropped back into your post so that you can add text, and adjust the sharing options.

Posting Place and Location Data

You can post data into Google+ via your mobile device and sometimes via the web application. To test this latter effort, I told Google+ to post my location from my Macbook Air, and it knew exactly which coffee shop I was sitting in (The Wired Monk, in Halifax, Nova Scotia, at the time of this writing, should you be the curious type).

Some people share place or location data so that they can encourage serendipitous meetings. You can have your sales team check in via location data to give your team a sense of their comings and goings, if that is of value to your organization. You can use location check-ins to mark potential prospects, for instance, if you were looking for places to sell your retail products. There are lots of ways to consider using place data as part of the value of Google+.

Other Post Options

You can go back and edit a post or delete a post after you've added it to the stream. Maybe you've accidentally sent out a link to all the public that shares your upcoming ad campaign's main website address. No worries. You can pull it down relatively fast. You can also link to the post by clicking the arrow in the upper-right corner of the post and selecting Link to This Post.

Here's a valuable option: You can report and remove offensive or spam-like comments. Thus, if you're posting about an inspiring speech your CEO gave, and someone comes along and decides your post is the perfect place to sell Christian Louboutin shoes, you have the power to report the comment as spam (and please do so), and then remove the comment from your post.

Be *very* clear about what you decide to remove from your comments. If you are Sony Electronics and someone from Kodak comes onto your post and talks about a competing camera, that's probably a moment worth discussing with your team before you make your next move. My professional advice would be to leave the comment as long as it's respectful. Your company policy might be different.

In a similar vein, say you represent the Alabama Power Company, and someone comes on to complain that his power bill is higher than ever before and that the power company stinks. This comment should be permitted to stay. It's an opinion, and it's not slanderous or otherwise. Instead, what should come soon after that comment is a response from someone at Alabama Power offering a phone call to review the customer's bill and seek an understanding of what might have happened or changed.

Deleting negative impressions of your company or organization has a negative impact, actually. In a survey I've long since forgotten the source of, I read that 70% of customers facing a web page that shows only positive impressions and reviews reported that something was "wrong," even though they couldn't always put their finger on the cause of this. This should be at the top of your priorities when deciding how to moderate comments on your posts.

Disabling Comments and Reshare

Now consider two more posting options. The first is whether you want to disable comments for a post. I've seen this used successfully when someone chooses to reshare someone else's post but wants the comments to fall into that original post and not end up on the shared post. Walk through an example.

Shilpa, the director of Consumer Experience, posts a video asking potential customers what they think of a new feature. Anil, the vice president of Research and Development, reshares Shilpa's post to his audience by pushing Share under the post after it comes up in his stream. Upon publishing that share, Anil rushes to the upper-right corner of the post and selects Disable Comments. He then puts text above the share of Shilpa's video that says, "Please comment on Shilpa's original post." People aren't *obligated* to click through and comment, obviously, but this encourages that outcome, at least.

The other option you can enable is to Lock This Post. This comes in handy, for instance, if you're sharing something with a select circle, such as your Community Managers circle, and you don't want the information going out into the general Google+ stream. Other times you might not want to share a post beyond the initial target circle because it's something you'd like to keep under wraps to some extent.

The Importance of Sharing

Chapter 9, "A Simple Content Strategy," talks about how all this stuff in this chapter can be used, and that includes building a practice of sharing other people's information. In Google+, similar to how Twitter used to work, sharing is an important part of the strategy.

For this chapter, the *how* of sharing is simple. Go to your home page—the little house with the buttons and lines below it—and pick which stream you'd like to read from. Or if you want to see everything, click the word Stream below your avatar on the left side. Then, when you find a post worth sharing, enabled to be shared, simply click the blue Share button beneath the post, and decide which of your circles you'd like to share it with. You can also share a post with the Public overall. Remember: If the original post was shared with a limited audience, then you can share it only with your circles, extended circles, and a limited audience, as well.

Why sharing is important is that people need to see more than your original posts. They need to understand that you're interested in sharing other people's information if it's germane to the story as well. For instance, if you're someone from Ford (oh, like Scott Monty), you have to share other people's posts about cars in general because the kinds of people who want to read about Ford probably also want to be kept up on industry news.

The coolest (and by "coolest," I mean the way that bosses will twitch, but it goes a long way in showing how human your company can be) way to share is to occasionally share the other company's information. For instance, if you're a publisher at Marvel Comics, it'd be nice to give DC a nod for winning an award for some Batman story or the like. For whatever reason, that Macy's vs Gimbels trick really goes a long way in showing people that you're not just in it to pitch your product.

8

Video, Hangouts, and More

YouTube, by several measures, rates as the second search engine in the world behind Google, but people rarely think of it as such. When I ask people who don't frequently use YouTube about what they think of the service, they say, "Oh, that's where the skateboarding dog videos are, right?" Well, yes, and there are billions of other videos you can also view. Because YouTube is owned by Google, the search feature works well, and you're able to find what you need.

I use YouTube as my instruction manual. If I buy a gadget, I can find someone who has already mastered every nuance and who has shot a video to help me use it. Companies should learn to embrace YouTube along with the people demonstrating how to use their products.

One of the complaints with YouTube is that it's not the easiest place to have a conversation. The comments section does not offer any mechanisms for community, or to follow up and do business. Let's discuss how Google+ is perfect for this issue!

Adding Video to Google+

After reading this book, think about the use of video in your business, and specifically, using a platform like Google+ (and YouTube by extension) to grow your business. I believe that video is so beneficial that I devoted a whole chapter to this subject. Are you with me?

There are 2.5 ways to use video in Google+. You can post YouTube video links into Google+. You can use Hangouts, which is a tool that connects up to 10 people live on video. And some of us (at the time of this writing) can host a Hangouts on Air, which is when you have a handful of video sources but broadcast to even more people. Let's discuss these ways while focusing on "why" to use them and what ways you can use them.

YouTube and Your Business

More and more people are turning to YouTube for information and perspective, and not just entertainment. Take the time to look up a product or a service that you're curious about, and see what you find. Look for your competitor's product. What is said about it? What has anyone posted about you?

No matter what you find, take note. If there are several videos complaining about your product, isn't that a great opportunity to fix the problem? If there aren't videos saying anything either way about what you're doing, is that telling? Note that it's not because your "customers aren't there." If there are more videos about your competitor's product, then there's more work for you to do, right?

When making videos for YouTube, keep them brief (under 2 minutes). Title your video using language that people would likely type into a search bar. For example, if you title a video "the P35R-920 mixer" and not "best mixer for making bread dough," then you're missing a great opportunity. If you feel the need, add the "P35R-920" tag somewhere at the end of the title.

You can create the following types of videos to help your business:

- How-to information about your specific product.

- Interviews with customers who use your product in unique ways.

- Information about the space you serve; that is, videos *not* about your product or service but about the environment in which that product serves (for example, if you sell running shoes, create a video about the technique of running).

• Testimonials and referrals from satisfied customers.

When thinking about live video, you might have a few more suggestions. Again, video is one of the most important, but least used functions of Google+ and the digital channel at large for business. With that said, let's talk about the opportunities for using Hangouts.

Hangouts and Your Business

There are two types of Hangouts. Smaller Hangouts connect you and up to nine other people for two-way conversations. Hangouts on Air is where you and up to nine other people can be viewed by an (nearly) unlimited group of viewers. There are many ways to consider using both types of Hangouts. Let's start with the two-way, up-to-10-people kind first.

• **Team meetings**—If your team is distributed across fewer than 10 locations, you can host team meetings via Google+ Hangouts. This enables you to use webcam sharing, screen sharing, group document editing, and more. You can make it private by setting the invite list to include specific people/accounts related to your team. Inviting "public" or "your circles" is not advisable.

• **Instruction**—You can offer how-to information or connect in person to help people better use your product or service. You can create a mix of published video (as discussed previously) or shoot live "office hours" to get people even deeper into the knowledge of your tools. I, for one, would love this for certain technologies and products that I use (poorly).

• **Tutoring**—Smaller or solo businesses can use this to great effect. With Hangouts, you can have up to nine people at once talking about your service or product; for example, you can offer nutrition courses or guitar lessons. If you're a life coach, you can use Hangouts for an "accountability group" to keep people on the same page. Note that you can charge for this service and restrict access based on payments.

When using Hangouts on Air, you must consider your business, no matter what it is, as a media company. What can you do with the power to broadcast live video to others? Answering this, obviously, is a great way to prepare yourself for what you can do with Hangouts on Air.

Figure 8-1   The Google+ Hangouts page.

In the first few months of its availability, Hangouts on Air was used for live music events, conversations between world leaders, and a presentation by President Barack Obama. In these instances, there were only one or two cameras live, and everyone else was able to watch as the audience. Here are a few ways you can use Hangouts on Air:

- **Corporate announcements and press events**—You can create Hangouts on Air to share news with the public. This is probably the first and simplest way to look at the potential for this service. Just as Dell's leader Michael Dell used straightforward Hangouts in the beginning, you now have the power to reach more people simultaneously.

- **Panel discussions**—Imagine including three or four guests as a host for a discussion on a topic of interest to your customers. For example, L.L. Bean can host a mix of wilderness guides, adventure sports professionals, and a wildlife expert while talking about next season's big adventures. Or a group of engineers can explain to potential partners how your system integrates with the rest of the world. The possibilities are endless.

- **Performance**—As discussed, the first uses of Hangouts on Air were for entertainment purposes. You can host a band, a stand-up comic, a keynote speaker, or whomever you think would garner you some attention from a grateful audience. Because it's a Hangout on Air environment, you can encourage questions from the viewers and provide related information in previous and subsequent posts, so that all the information is collected neatly in one spot.

There are many more ways to use Hangouts and Hangouts on Air, but these suggestions should get you thinking. Let's switch gears a little and talk about some fairly tactical information when creating video of any kind. Although this is not a how-to guide, the following sections provide helpful tips to save you time.

Creating Video

If you need to record video to be uploaded to YouTube at a later time, or if you want to work on a live presentation, consider the following:

- You can use any type of camera, and not just the one built into your laptop or desktop computer. Provided your computer can see the attached camera, it works just as well, and maybe even better than the camera that shipped with your computer.

- The biggest problem with video is poor audio. Most people either record from a loud environment, record or present too far away from the microphone, or set the microphone levels too high or low. Test your settings before you begin a video. Interviewing an amazing guest or CEO for 40 minutes and then realizing that you had the microphone switched off is a hideous thing (I've done it about 3,434,917 times).

- After audio comes lighting as a video culprit. Unless you want to disguise the identity of the subject you're filming, put the light in front of him or her, and not behind. Recording next to your bright office windows with you in front creates a silhouette experience. For more information on this subject, perform a Google search for "3 point lighting."

- When recording video, brevity rules. (I discuss this point several times, but it's because people rarely follow this advice.) The suggested length of a video for consumption on YouTube is around 2 minutes or less in length. Yes, interviews tend to last longer. When editing the video, consider creating a "highlight reel" or "best of" video for people who want a longer footage.

- When editing video, keep it simple. Easy-to-use programs include iMovie for a Mac or Windows Movie Maker for a PC. Don't use too many fancy transitions or effects. These options might be fun to work with, but too many of them will make your video look amateur. Stay simple—everyone involved will appreciate it more.

- In setting up a one-on-one interview, get closer to the person than you'd expect. No matter what type of camera you use, set up your shot so that you (or the interviewer) are fairly close to the subject. In my experience, knees touching (though maybe not on camera) is close enough. (Yes, it feels awkward, but it gets the shot you're looking for, as it turns out.)

- One way to "salvage" an interview that runs too long and too loose is to edit the video with a host or announcer narrating and setting up "bits" from the interview, so that you can cut and edit as needed. I asked Steve Garfield about his work with the Boston Media Makers, and he said, "Then, cut to a snip of what Steve Garfield said, instead of the whole deal."

- The best way to practice looking natural in front of the camera is to record yourself often in front of the camera. The more you do this and don't publish the results, the more you can learn, practice, and improve how you come off in front of the camera. Look directly into the lens as if you're addressing one person. If you find it difficult to look into the lens, you can always tape a pair of eyes (like a cut-out picture of eye-balls) directly above the lens in which to focus.

- The best way to eliminate the "umms" from your language is to pause instead of saying "um." If you want to edit the video or cut the awkward pauses, it will be much simpler than removing the "um" sounds.

Everything else will come with time and experience. The more you practice, the better things will be. The more you make mistakes, the better your video will be.

Nearly as important as creating your own video and Hangouts is the world of curation. If you curate video from other sources and present these to your audience as well, you come off as someone who shares useful information no matter the source, instead of someone who promotes only your products and services. Curation is every bit as important as creation. For as many times as I've gone in search of a company's official videos, I've quite often found something just as useful (or better) created by someone who spent time figuring it out. Yes, YouTube is my instruction manual. Bring this mindset to Google+ and you have a winner. So, what will your video be about?

9

A Simple Content Strategy

No matter what your primary business is, you are a publishing company in the new world of social media and social networks. You might be the owner of a small (but growing) restaurant chain in Milwaukee, Wisconsin, but if you aren't posting pictures of your delicious custom burgers to your Facebook group, your Twitter feed, and your Google+ stream, you're spending far too much money on advertising—or you have plenty of empty tables.

From the largest companies to the smallest, people realize the importance of creating interesting content that engages specific audiences via these social channels. Attend BlogHer even once, and you can see that the "mommy blogger" universe is being courted by the biggest companies out there. Companies such as Disney do spectacular work integrating bloggers and podcasters into their events as press. (I attended the inaugural voyage of the Disney Dream cruise ship.)

But creating compelling content is difficult, takes time, and requires some consideration for this new world. Simply blasting the same message to Facebook, LinkedIn, your email list, and everywhere else won't cut it. Furthermore, if all you do is post about your business, people will tune out quickly, especially if that sharing comes from the individual accounts. Finally, if you are going to invest all this time in creating and also sharing content, it better be with the intent to build some kind of lasting business result. So, what should you do? This chapter helps you answer this question.

How Others Approach Content Sharing

Before going into how to create content, check out some samplings of how business people use Google+. This illustrates a few important points, suggests a few reasons why you might emulate something these people do, and shows you more than one way to look at it. None of the commentary provided here has been vetted by these people. These are my opinions and insights into their choices and postings.

Jennifer Cisney (Kodak)

I visited the stream of Jennifer Cisney, Kodak's Chief Blogger. On the day that I took a peek, she had created four posts:

- She shared another person's post about giving away dog books and cookies.

- She shared an article about a genetic portrait series.

- She shared an article about a photo project showing different living situations for children.

- She shared a poster she designed for an event she planned to attend.

Jennifer's posts ask nothing of the person reading them. She's not asking people to rush to Kodak and buy a Playsport camera. Several days of posts reveal that she rarely mentions Kodak projects or products directly on Google+. However, she shares lots of great posts about photography, interesting photography projects, and other things she's passionate about. Her work made me want to grab my own camera to try some of these projects.

That's the magic. Jennifer isn't paid to sell directly. She's paid to inspire the community, to keep a warm brand sentiment around Kodak and its involvement in pictures and memories, and to just be a good digital citizen.

You can't read Jennifer's stream and not know she's a dog lover. You can't read what she shares and not realize that she's into photography. You never get the feeling that she's there to pitch you something. I think that's a great way to approach content sharing, if you're looking for a strong, warm brand sentiment.

Michael Dell (CEO, Dell)

On the day I visited Michael Dell's stream, he shared the following:

- He shared another person's post that talked about a great Hangout they shared (and thanked the person).

- He hung out with 21 people. (I don't know the subject matter of this.)

- He shared reactions to HP's exit from the PC market.

- He wished HP goodbye in the PC world.

The day I sampled was pertinent to Michael's core business. One of his key competitors threw in the towel. He stated his continued support of that same space. He pointed to analysts' remarks to strengthen his position. But more interestingly and more telling, he also spent time in a Hangout (probably talking about this), and he stuck around to thank some people for their participation in it.

Michael shares almost entirely Dell-specific information. I checked a few other days and found most of the posts related to his business. In contrast to Jennifer Cisney, I know nothing about Michael, except that he is clearly passionate about his business (and one would hope he is) and that he is active in Google+.

Neither of these approaches is wrong, by the way. I think Michael's approach makes him seem accessible, and I see his interest in features such as the Hangout as sure signs that he intends to use this service for company communication that goes off-script, or at least enables some candid interaction. I find it encouraging and exciting

Scott Monty (Ford Motor Company)

Scott's the head of social media for Ford. He handles this primarily in a communications role, like the "people's PR," in my perspective. On the day I visited Scott's stream, he did the following:

- Reshared the +Ford Motor Company account's breaking news.

- Commented on the difference between comments on Facebook and comments on Google+ in reaction to the news. (He thought Facebook had more negative opinions.)

On another day, Scott did the following:

- Shared a local event's news

- Pointed out a competitor's bad news

On other days, Scott participates with the community, asking for thoughts and advice, shares information that strengthens the use of Google+, and spreads general good will. My take on Scott's use is that he does a lot to promote Ford in a positive way and discusses other industry news in addition to local Michigan news, which helps create local pride, something that certainly matters to Ford.

The majority of the information he shared were links to other articles, but he also created unique posts, especially when posting questions. Like Michael Dell, Scott goes to the community at Google+ to get its take, although Scott tends to comment back and forth with people on his posts, whereas Michael tends to do that in video only (from what I could see).

Bill Gerth (Social Media Lead at Comcast)

Bill has inherited the mantle left by Frank Eliason, who famously put Comcast on the social media map for his work on Twitter with @comcastcares. I've spoken with Bill a few times on Twitter but had not seen his Google+ profile. Because Comcast did so well (and got so much positive media attention) for its Twitter work, I thought I'd see how Bill uses Google+.

Over the course of several days, Bill shared articles about social media and an interesting photo or two. He twice pointed to Comcast in those several days, helping people by reminding them to upgrade their Xfinity TV applications. Overall, his information was interesting for social media types, but it's clear he still does most of his "work" on Twitter and not on Google+.

The Biggest Content Difference (So Far) on Google+ for Business Users

Looking at another dozen business professionals using Google+, at this point, the biggest difference is that most people share more personal or indirectly related-to-business posts on Google+ than they do on other social networks.

On Twitter, Jennifer Cisney is @KodakCB, and her stream is quite actively sharing the Kodak story. Her Twitter avatar and background are branded Kodak, and most of the tweets relate to her business.

On Twitter, Michael Dell is @MichaelDell, and his background is branded with pictures of his company's products. He tweets nothing but Dell-specific or PC industry-specific information.

On Twitter, Scott Monty is @ScottMonty, and his avatar and background are branded Ford. He shares a lot of customer service and communications help. He talks conversationally to people answering Ford Motor Company product and service questions. He's personable but still sticks closely to Ford topics.

On Twitter, Bill Gerth is @ComcastBill (also @ComcastCares), and he is 100% customer service-driven. His entire stream reads of @replies to customers with issues he's helping to resolve. All tweets that I observed over a few days were work-related.

So then, what should you do? Should you stick to mostly personal information on Google+? Should you keep your business on Facebook and Twitter? Should you alter your content strategy for Google+?

Although everyone's mileage may vary, I have a sense of what might work to blend that personal touch with a business agenda. The following sections include some ideas for building a stream on Google+ that might help you build the relationships that can lead to business. These examples are for different types of businesses.

Restaurant Owner

If you're in the restaurant business, you want to show that your place is *the* place to be. Your goal is to attract people, to show them what your restaurant is about, and to entice them to come down. Now, *most* restaurants stuff their social network streams with coupons and offers. Why? Because that's how they advertise in other media. Well, here's a chance to do something new. Try these ideas:

- **Post photos:** People want to see your place and want to see happy faces and delicious dishes. (When shooting photos of people, always ask for their permission to post them on the web.) Showing off your great meals help people see what they will get when they come in.

- **Share video:** Interview the chef (if she is the kind of person who would sell your restaurant), your best bartender, or whoever can help you sell what makes your restaurant better. Make the video's duration under 2 minutes. Upload it to YouTube, and post it to your stream for people to get an even better flavor of the restaurant.

- **Share local news (positive, mostly):** You'll hear me say this a lot for businesses that have location in mind. Be the hub of your community. This shows people that you care about more than your restaurant.

- **Share posts:** If you know any other local Google+ users, share their posts occasionally, especially if they promote something of their own or sharing an accomplishment. The more you help them celebrate themselves, the more they'll come to interact with you when the time is right.

For a restaurant, you don't need to post too many new things each day. Between two to three posts a day total (including sharing other people's news and stories) is probably enough. However, you need to pay close attention to the comments on items you post. People will interact with you, and how you approach commenting back and forth can have an impact on how people perceive you and the restaurant.

Community Manager/Developer

A common role in companies these days has to do with embracing and engaging the community around company products and services. Different companies treat this role differently. Kodak, for instance, has Jennifer Cisney as its Chief Blogger, which is ultimately a community role. Scott Monty is Ford's head of social media, so he has a community role for at least part of his responsibilities. It's handled differently at Dell and Comcast, where many people have their hands in the community and it's a shared function. No matter how your company does it, the following are some ways you should approach creating content for your community:

- Talk *about* your community. If you're Ford Motor Company, show people who are excited about their Focus Hybrids. If you're Kodak, show off photos your users have taken with your products. Talk about them, not you, though.

- Post information that's useful to that community. If you create project management software, share articles about better ways to manage meetings. If you're a soap company, share posts about how to make an at-home spa experience.

- Share photos of community members. If you host face-to-face events, make a point of asking permission to post photos of the event on the web, and then share photos from your big unveiling party or your customer appreciation day event. The more people who see themselves, or people just like them, the better.

- Share how-to information about your products and services. If you sell cooking supplies, offer recipes. If you sell legal services, maybe you can share best practices about how to prepare for a meeting with your team.

The number of posts for a community manager type should be more frequent than it might be for most other roles. This is because the community manager encourages community engagement. However, a caveat exists: Don't post garbage. If you have nothing interesting to post, don't waste the attention in people's streams.

Comments by community manager types are usually the bread and butter of experiences. If you look at Scott Monty's posts, you can see that he engages a lot of time in the comments section. On Facebook, I observed that he was equally as active. On Twitter, Bill Gerth and the @comcastcares team is quite active. They use it as a customer service channel.

Comments show your buyers that you care about their opinions. Comments give your customer a voice. They allow you to speak off-message and yet bolster the message. They also show a very human side to your business, and this is worth its weight in gold.

That's one last detail I'd like to bring up: Community management as a role is a strange mix. It's part promotional (using PR and communications), part marketing (sharing offers and deals), and a strong part of customer service (helping customers get what they need). If you do only one of these three functions, you're not likely serving your customers or users in the best way.

Online Store

If you're the owner of an online (or online-mostly) store, using a service such as Google+ is a great way to be the "online shopkeeper" outside of your e-commerce-heavy environment. If you think of your store as a well-tuned system that helps guide people toward closing a purchase, you wouldn't want to blur that with too much social networking interaction. (Although you might consider installing the Google +1 button on all your products.) Therefore, if you spend some time on social networks such as Google+, you might find people to interact with who might be seeking what you sell. The following are ideas for the type of content the online store owner might post:

- Post product demos of things you sell, if that makes sense. If video would create a better demonstration, post video. If not, post photos.

- Post interesting ideas or serving suggestions for your products. If you sell pens, show interesting art made by the pens.

- Post profiles and interviews with the owners. The more people see who's behind the store, the more trust they'll feel in making purchases. You buy from people you "know," even if your mind sometimes stretches that "know" a little bit.

- It might be interesting to try live product demonstrations in Hangouts. A video I shot of my favorite carry-on bag amounted to more than 50 sales and counting via affiliate marketing. You might find similar success selling via a Hangout.

In most cases, your time on Google+ doesn't need to be long to be effective. You might post information early in your day and then again later in your day, taking time to see whether you receive any comments or reactions to the posts. You might also search Google+ (via Google: just put in site:plus.google.com and then enter your search terms, and you might find people talking about the items you sell). That could yield even better results, but be wary of seeming to spam people. A fine line exists between helping and jumping in and seeming creepy.

Professional Speaker or Thought Leader

For those professional speakers and thought leaders who want to get potential clients via social networks such as Google+, what helps people select you is a blend of traits. People want to know that you're professional. They want to know that you're intelligent. They might want to know that you're personable, or at least what type of personality you have. They probably wouldn't mind seeing if what you share is interesting to them and their business needs.

Be willing to share more of your personality than your serious side, though. I see business consultants and professionals throw up their avatars in their best suit or dress, sharing only specific and pertinent information. It doesn't hurt to show a bit of your lighter side. Following are some guidelines:

- If you're a blogger, share your best posts, maybe not *all* your posts. If people subscribe to your blog, they probably won't want the double-dip of you sharing it with them.

- Post YouTube videos of your speeches or seminars. Seeing you in action is a great way to lure people into wanting to hire you for work. Be sure to post a link to your contact page when posting a video, so that they don't just watch and comment.

- Share other people's posts that are pertinent to your main industry. There's an importance to this step. If you post only your own items or posts about how great you are, it comes off that way, and people don't want that. They want you to seem like a participant in the conversation, not a solo act.

A professional in this category might post three to five times a day, and paying attention to the comments is also important. Getting people back to your main site or blog is equally important. Having all the conversation on the social network robs your blog of potential social proof, meaning that comments that normally would show up on your blog posts will live on Google+, and that's not your real estate.

One last thought to professionals seeking to drum up connections on Google+: As you consider your sharing and posting strategy, be sure to keep that mix of off-topic material in there. The moment you seem like a "stuffed shirt," you'll find more resistance to what you do choose to share. It just happens that way.

Writer, Photographer, and Artist

Many "tribes" of creatives use Google+ to the fullest. Photographers share many of their works because the platform has nice aesthetics for sharing and a simple commenting system. Writers share bits of upcoming projects and also seek advice or pointers to research information. Artists connect with all kinds of new people who appreciate their work. In all cases, I'd recommend posting items in the following categories:

- Share what you can of upcoming projects. Even if you're sworn to secrecy, showing a few photos or a quick video clip of you at the drawing board can excite. You might not think it's exciting because you're used to sitting there working for hours and hours, but others might get a thrill.

- Post quick video interviews talking about whatever you can about your methods, your styles, your influences, and so on.

- Start a Hangout and invite people in to ask you questions. (At the time I was writing this part of the book, I noticed that comics and film writer Greg Pak was taking questions in a simple text post. I thought of just how much more fun it would be to do as a video Hangout.)

- Post questions for research, and maybe even invite people to contribute to projects, if it makes sense. Collaborations via this medium are quite easy and potentially full of exciting new possibilities because of the scale of the active audience, plus the diversity of locations of people.

Writers, photographers, artists, and other creatives have a lot of potential with Google+. It's not necessarily as deep a niche as several other sites that cater to a group. Flickr, for instance, has millions more passionate photography users. deviantART has a huge art community. There are many writing communities. And yet, people explore Google+ as an interesting crossroads between those more single-serving communities and the more general public. (Not that I consider Google+ a decent representation of the general public yet, but I think it is more general than niche sites.)

Posting to Build Connections

One point not covered is the notion of posting and sharing simply to build connections. For instance, perhaps you use Google+ as a way to meet with interesting people because those types of people drive your own creativity or fuel your own vision. People can fall into this category in many different ways: investors, artists, analysts, writers, journalists, and so on. In all cases, my advice is the same:

- Share interesting posts from outside of Google+ and from sources that aren't as typically sourced. For instance, if you're into technology, sharing something originally posted on Mashable or TechCrunch won't likely get you noticed on Google+. However, pointing out an interesting gadget you saw on uncrate.com might get you some interesting new followers.

- Post original content that takes a completely different view than the norm. For instance, when people were giving their thanks and praise to Steve Jobs upon hearing his announcement that he was stepping down as CEO of Apple, if your post wrote up a dissenting view, it would no doubt receive a lot of traffic. (Perhaps all of it angry, but you'd certainly get attention.)

- Find off-topic posts of interest. Curiosities are most definitely what help someone connect. Perhaps you have a knowledge of interesting cover songs, so you share Karen Souza's rendition of Radiohead's "Creep" via a YouTube video. It's a heck of a lot more interesting than sharing the Richard Cheese version and might lead to a new connection—or ten.

And why would you want all kinds of connections? Some people find value in a lot of eclectic connections because they lead those people to a more diverse network. Others like more connections because they seek to do something with the value of the volume. (That's how advertising works, for instance.) Still others just like to find connections for all the varied interests. If you're into bird-watching, yodeling, and mixed martial arts fights, it's going to take a little work to find and create those circles, so you might as well post eclectic and varied content to try and connect with those who share your interests.

Value Your Audience's Attention

Above all else, value your audience's attention. The more "junk" you throw at them, the less they will pay attention. Cherish their interaction. Comment back when they comment. (Not necessarily for every comment you get, but be the #1 commenter in your own stream.) The more you value your audience, the more value they can bring you. It's as simple as that.

10

The "Warm" Sell

All along, the secret of this book has been this: It's not about the technology. Lance Armstrong said it first: It's not about the bike. What he meant was that his determination, practice, focus, and preparation drove him. What I mean is simpler still: Using Google+ for business is about understanding how to build human relationships; it is not about this specific technology.

In this case, you can "paint" in this medium called Google+ because it gives you access to millions of potential new clients, has benefits for how people can find you using Google's search functions, and affords you a way to create interactions that can (hopefully) lead to sustainable business.

This requires something called the "warm" sell. If you've picked up this book with the intention to learn a few magic formulas that you can automate, set, and forget, and then sit back while the money flows into your bank account, you might be disappointed. However, you learn how Google+ can help you build connections and how you might sell to them.

To that end, let's start with some of the philosophy and mindset behind how Google+ can best help you sell, and then see some tangible examples of what you can do with this information. Some might not fit your particular business model, but see what you can do to adapt them. Most are reasonably universal, but tuned for a Google+ world.

Attention Is a Gift

Attention is a gift. People choose to circle you and pay attention to your posts on Google+. It's completely opt-in. That means that if you spam them with sales offers all the time, they will tune you out. They will either uncircle you or click the Ignore button, thus blocking any further chances to build a relationship.

With that in mind, you should post a mix of business-specific information and information that's helpful to the community. Don't flood the stream with dozens of posts a day. (This often earns you a transfer to circles that people name things such as Noisy or Blabbermouths.) Instead, think strategically about the mix of posts that might help convey your interest in empowering your potential buyer, plus a call to action here and there.

Make It About Them

The more you post information that empowers or highlights your prospective buyers, the more likely people will respond and react to your information. The more it's about you, the easier it is to tune you out. Remember, those amazing new products you create aren't amazing until your customers find that your products changed their lives. Even if you sell toilet lids, you need to make your interactions on Google+ about how these toilet lids can make your buyers' lives amazing.

Turn Self-Promotion into Appreciation

If you win an award, make the thanks point toward your buyers. Any time you brag, it turns people off. It doesn't matter that you're so proud of making the *New York Times* Bestseller list. If you don't write your post about that to read "Thank YOU for making this book successful," people tune you out. Attention is a gift. Appreciate the hell out of your community.

Don't Waste Chances to Sell

On the other side of the coin, realize that you're on Google+ for a reason, and if that reason is business, business is based on converting prospects into buyers, and turning buyers into loyal members of the community. Even if someone has purchased, love them as a loyal customer. If someone's on the fence, give them all the help you can. If they're not yet even a prospect, educate them about the space, and include the occasional pointer back to what you're doing.

Think in terms of how you might add value to the other person's interactions with you. That's where the sales come from—more about that in a moment. Just realize that you're here to sell, but that selling doesn't mean every sentence you write on Google+ is about driving someone to buy.

The Warm Sell—Warming Up a Sale

Say I want to sell a webinar about how to use Google+. (I've done that a few times, you should know.) I would do a series of posts something like the following.

- Post interesting free information about Google+.

- Post a few off-topic posts that also point to how Google+ is interesting.

- Post starter guides that people can run with.

- Post video screencasts showing off some tricks and tips (all free).

- Accumulate a bunch of these free posts.

- Write a post offering a paid webinar for a deeper dive, including a list of skills people can learn from the experience, and end with a link to the buying page.

In the post offering the paid webinar, write copy that speaks entirely from the buyer's perspective. It might be something like this:

"You've been using Google+ for a little while now, and you've heard that people are having success with using it for business, but you haven't exactly hit it out of the park yet. You've figured out some of the basics, but nothing seems to be moving the needle for you. If you're interested in learning how to use Google+ to build business relationships and improve your sales and marketing efforts, reserve your seat for this informative tutorial on how to build business using Google+."

Something like this that includes bullet points about specific takeaways works. Also, end with a Reserve Your Seat link that takes people to a sales page.

This is how I would do it, and I should be clear that I have a reputation in the space that I wrote about here and that people know me for this kind of information. What if you're a lot less known, and what if the people who have opted to circle you don't yet know you enough to trust you as a business leader? And what if your product is a little more difficult to sell? Now look at those premises, too.

Getting to Know You

If you join Google+ and somehow convince a bunch of people to circle you to follow your posts, and the first thing you do is offer them products or services to buy, you'll quickly be uncircled. A little bit of warming up is necessary.

Take the community-minded approach. If you sell special soaps, your buyers are primarily women, primarily people who like to pamper themselves, and people with some discretionary income. To build community around that, share other items that would be of interest to that demographic. For instance, share posts about inspiring books, posts about new trends in beauty, and other topics not directly related to the soap you sell, but related to the buyers you're courting.

Make sure your About page on your profile is complete. Tell people exactly who you are. Give them pictures of you. Make sure they have ample ways to contact you. The more people can feel that they understand who you are, what you stand for, what you believe in, the more they can identify with you.

Another point about helping people get to know you is that the more you comment on your prospects' posts (and never in a way that's selling your stuff—unless it's *exactly* what they're asking about), the more they will feel a connection to you that can help you help them in the future.

The Difficult Sell

I bought my car on the Internet. The story is useful to explain how social networks can help you build a sale. I'll talk you through the story to see if there are nuggets of information that can help you, should you be selling something a little more complex than books, energy bars, or software.

Aaron Manley Smith runs a virtual car dealership called Motorphilia. He used to sell quite heavily through eBay but has since expanded to building business on Facebook and now also Google+. I met him once at an event in Austin, Texas, and found his story interesting, but I also filed it in the "But I'm not looking for a car, and Aaron seems to sell mostly exotic cars" file.

Then, one day, I thought I'd search around to find a new Chevy Camaro SS. I looked at my local car dealership websites and found them terribly lacking. They basically are all built to have you come in for a test drive. There's not enough information on the site. The pricing wasn't posted. It was just a mess.

So, I did what any blogger would do: I wrote a blog post complaining about it. I wrote "Dear Car Dealerships: Your Website Sucks." In the post, I explained how buyers have changed how they buy, and that most of the websites I visited were old school and that it was dissuading me from making a purchase.

The blog post found its way onto Facebook, and within 4 minutes of seeing it, Aaron Manley Smith sent me a message via Facebook saying that he'd located exactly the car I had mentioned in the blog post, and that if I sent him $1,000 via PayPal, he'd acquire it for me. (Yes, this is a Facebook story, but this was a year before Google+ had come out. The same details translate handsomely to G+.)

I did it. I sent Aaron the money. A handful of days later, I had a brand new Camaro that cost me about $5,000 less than the dealership up the street, with no haggling, no fuss, and I did it completely over the Internet.

But what goes into performing a complex sale like that? Here's where there might be some learning from how Aaron does what he does that you can take into your sales methods. Again, your mileage may vary, but realize that these nuggets can be adapted for your interests. Now go behind the scenes on the details I didn't explain by considering the following:

- **Social proof:** First, Aaron mastered the art of social proof. If you look at the Motorphilia fan page on Facebook, it is post after post of interesting cars (for enthusiasts), plus it's a bunch of photos and posts congratulating recent customers on their cars. Aaron makes the buyer the star, but at the same time, he is subtly pointing out every sale he makes with photos and videos.

- **Behind the scenes:** Aaron sends photos from car auctions he and his team attend, plus he shares interesting car pictures that keep his audience happy. He also shares bits of himself on Google+ that have nothing to do with cars and Motorphilia. The more you get to know him, the more you feel like you trust him (without having ever shaken his hand across a table).

- **Referrals:** Because of how Aaron does his work, and because he uses social networks extensively to promote and show off the sales he's made, the people who he sells cars to do a great job of referring business to him by talking and posting about the experience. I've written blog posts about Aaron. I bring him up in speeches. And now, I've written about him in this book. Referrals are gold for most complex sales. (You in the real estate profession just nodded, right?)

- **Presence:** Aaron is active on more than a few social networks. It's serving him well in lieu of advertising because people get to know him in between their needs, plus his buyers are mostly on social networks. Because Aaron has tuned his sales methods specifically to social network users, maintaining a presence here makes sense. (Before you start saying, "But my buyers aren't on social networks," the Pew Internet and American Life Project reported in August 2011 that half of U.S. adults regularly use social networking sites. I don't have stats for other countries, but it varies per country, obviously.)

There's a lot to digest in this segment, but I think it bears consideration. Building trust to accomplish a big sale takes time, but if you're doing difficult sales, you already have a sense of the duration of the sales cycle. If I told you that social networks are just another tool like the phone and face-to-face visits to try and land a sale, you'll think more about how that slots into your other methods, and you'll allot time accordingly.

If you want some further reading to complement what Aaron has accomplished, check out John Jantsch's *The Referral Engine*. It's packed with information that can benefit your attempts to emulate some of the best of what Aaron has done.

Affiliate Marketing and Google+

I've seen some early examples of people using Google+ for affiliate marketing (selling other people's products for a financial reward). Most of the early examples have been the terrible spammy variety. Luckily, Google+ has lots of good tools to enable people to report spam and to block people who take this approach. But those are the "bad guys." How can you use Google+ for affiliate marketing if you sell to a community that actually is interested in the products you sell. Consider these ideas:

- **Content sells:** If you promote travel gear, share good travel videos, and maybe add links to products you think would help out such a trip. In every case, be sure to disclose that what you promote is an affiliate link. (This is the law in the United States, but it's good practice everywhere.) You can just post the link and then put the affiliate link right after the link. That makes it simple.

- **Add something:** My friend and PodCamp co-founder, Christopher S. Penn, used to help his company sell student loans, and the way he did it was to create the Financial Aid Podcast. Every episode (and there were hundreds of them) had a mix of interesting links for college students, including free music, ideas on how to build a good resume, and all kinds of things that had nothing to directly do with financial aid. And yet, that information built trust, kept people listening, and gave Chris multiple opportunities to promote student loans. He made his company millions from this effort.

- **Don't sell 100% of the time:** Post content that relates to your community in between sales. To skip that step risks you being uncircled or ignored.

- **Help others sell:** If you want a magic trick in affiliate marketing, help others sell. Some programs actually offer two-tiered affiliate relationships, which means that you can recruit people and also make a cut off their sales. However, do it just because it can help your sales. This might mean resharing someone else's affiliate promotion. It might mean teaching people your best tips for selling. When you're helpful to others, they tend to reciprocate.

- **Try a hangout:** What if you did a live hangout showing off the product or service you're thinking of selling. Think QVC for the social network crowd. And before you poo-poo that idea as terrible, realize that QVC and related platforms get millions and millions of unit sales a week from doing simple promotional video coverage. A hangout would be a more intimate version of this—and definitely worth considering.

It's early to know whether Google+ will be useful for affiliate marketers, but anywhere that millions of people gather, there will be people testing whether it's of value. I think that making sure you sell in a human, relationship-minded way is always useful, and the platform certainly offers many ways to augment the methods you might use to sell.

Remember that the people who have joined Google+ haven't joined to buy things. They use this social network for many different purposes. Simply pushing sales into their stream would be a less successful method, so think accordingly.

The Two-Tier Sale

Another way to use Google+ to build sales is to not push for a sale right out of the gate. For instance, if you're a real estate professional, most people aren't actively seeking your services on any given day. However, when the time comes that they want to make a move or sell their place, you want to be top of mind. But nearly every business opportunity is like this. If you push directly for the sale and it's the wrong time, you risk falling under the waves and not being top of mind when the person *is* ready to buy. Therefore, you might encourage a sustained relationship before the sale in many ways.

Encourage subscriptions to your weekly email newsletter. Remember that Google+ is "rented" space. If the rules change, if something catastrophic happens, if the trends shift such that it's no longer the most amazing place to network, you'll lose all the work you've put into relationship building, if you have all your eggs in that basket. To that point, make efforts to invite people to get your weekly newsletter, where you control the mailing list, so that you have sustained access to those people. Ninety-three percent of people still prefer email to any other method to have a relationship with a brand, according to a study from Citi. Oh, and if you're not producing a useful, interesting, personable weekly email newsletter, you're missing a powerful part of your sales potential.

Another way to look at this is to consider Google+ as your warm networking in between sales calls. Sales people often look for ways to connect with their prospects in between pushes to move the sale along. For instance, if you sell something huge such as data center equipment, the cycle to buy might be 18 months or more.

While everything is coming together, another great way to use Google+ is to simply stay in touch and talk about whatever else is going on in your buyer's world. The more contact you have without pushing hard on the sale, the more your buyers can see you as someone who cares and shares value. (A great resource for this is the book *The Trusted Advisor* by David Maister and Charles Green. Pick it up to get more ideas on how this concept works.)

A Power Move—Mention Your Competitor

Following is one of those ideas that's a bit controversial, and that most bigger companies struggle to deal with. There might be times when your competitor's product or service is the better fit for someone. It takes a lot of guts to bring that up. However, ask yourself this: If the prospect is actually a better fit for the competitor's product, why not mention that product? You're not losing a sale. You are, however, building some trust.

A variation on this is to congratulate your competitor for wins from time to time. This runs counter to what most organizations want. However, think of it from the buyer's perspective. Every time you say something positive, it shows that you're a positive force, and it translates to goodwill.

You might be clear with the leadership, however, if you decide to take this approach and you're not the owner of the company. It's a bit of a fine line kind of move and isn't necessarily condoned at most companies. (And yet, it's so powerful and worth mentioning.)

If You're Not Directly in Sales

I have a little piece I do during some of my speeches to companies. I ask the audience, "How many of you are in sales?" Usually, a handful of people put up their hands. I then say, "Wrong. You're *all* in sales." And I believe this. No matter your role in the company, and no matter how large or small the company is, I believe that everyone is responsible for sales. If you're a customer service representative, your job is to sell the satisfaction of the buyer. If you're in public relations, your job is to sell people on the story of your company. If you're in finance, your job is to help improve margin as best as you can.

Sales is a big term. We all sell something every day—even if it's our opinion. I might sell you on going to see *Transformers 8*. You might sell me on checking out that new sushi restaurant. We sell ideas, thoughts, sentiments, and more, every day.

But related to actual sales—money-changing-hands sales—we all have a part to play in it. Scott Monty and Jennifer Cisney do not get measured on purchases made via their efforts, but those efforts most certainly keep the company in the better graces of their buyers. Greg Pak is measured as a writer by the success of his comic book sales (as one example), and his personable way to connect with people on Google+ turns people into buyers. That's the key—that's the value.

Quite a few people have a bit of a negative bias toward sales and salespeople. It's based on experiences with bad salespeople, however. Because the real trick is that the best salespeople make it seem like we wanted what we bought, and that we are smarter for knowing that.

For instance, the best servers in restaurants ask you whether you're a key lime pie fan or a chocolate molten lava cake fan. They don't ask you if you've "saved room for dessert." The difference is that they've already boxed you into an either-or decision that still has you thinking about selecting one of those two options, and when you *do* pick chocolate molten lava cake, you feel as if it were your own decision to make, and it was.

When you do it right, that's how sales feel to your buyer. You know what it feels like when you do it wrong. And again, if you're not directly in sales, you are still part of the sales process. There's more to consider here than an actual dollar-for-dollar interaction.

11

Growing an Audience

The question I'm asked more than any other question is how did I get such a big following on Twitter (and then Google+). Most times, people ask this question expecting some kind of software involvement, or some tool, or some formula. The best I can offer is a kind of formula:

- *Share interesting and useful information.*
- *Share information that's more about your audience than it is about you.*
- *Share more about other people than you share about yourself.*
- *Promote others more than you promote yourself.*
- *Comment as often as you can on other people's posts.*
- *Comment as often as you can on people's comments on your posts.*

If you stop reading now, you'd know what I know about growing an audience. Only, I owe lots of words and I have to give you something to chew on, so here goes. There's a bit more to it, obviously, but that formula is actually what I do.

Quality over Quantity

Whenever I talk about audience in an open forum such as Google+, at least two people per post say, "But it's quality and not quantity." These people are almost invariably graphic designers or customer service representatives. They are never from sales, marketing, or finance because those organizations understand the simple math of sample size versus response versus committed sale.

Yes, it's not that useful to build a huge audience if the majority of them aren't responsive and don't interact with your posts. For reading and interacting, it's much better to be prudent with your choices about whom you follow. Connect only with those people who add value and enrich your online experience. If you want to sell something, that is rarely a luxury you have.

You need to have an audience of some size so that you can continue telling the story, spreading the word, seeking relationships, and ultimately influence sales. Cold and simple—having a larger audience helps this effort.

Measuring the Size of Your Audience

The number you're looking for resides on your Circles page, up at the top, and it looks like Figure 11-1.

Figure 11-1 The size of your audience.

At the time of writing this book, 41,504 people added me to their circles, meaning that they opted in to receive my posts. I've circled 1,455 people. This is partially because I'm selective about who I follow on this social network and because Google+ has a 5,000-person following limit. I'd like to hold on to those slots for as long as I can.

Who puts you in a circle is the number you're looking at to determine your audience. In addition, you can track how many shares and +1s your comments get. These are "in-system" metrics, meaning that they mean something while you're inside Google+, but they don't translate directly to typical marketing metrics. The number of people who have you in circles on Google+ is not the same as the number of people in your email prospects list.

> People can choose to circle you and then choose to ignore your posts. This is worth knowing, but it's not worth worrying much about. You'll know by your level of engagement whether people pay any attention to you after they comment on a post of yours or share it.

Google+ makes it even more interesting to consider the size of your audience with its Extended Circles, which are the circles of the people you've added to your circles. Please don't close the book. I'll explain.

If you are Dave and you have circled Shashi, when you select to share information with your Extended Circles, what you're saying is, "Share this piece of information with anyone in Shashi's circles, too." However, this ends up showing up in Shashi's friends' "Incoming" stream, which isn't a widely read part of Google+.

Trying to measure the true reach and audience behind your posts and efforts on Google+ is difficult. If you want to keep an eye on a number for tracking purposes, track the following:

- People who have you in circles
- Number of comments per post
- Number of +1's per post
- Number of shares per post

For out-of-system metrics, you must determine whether calls to action are part of your posting strategy (talked about in previous chapters) and then specifically track from that. If you use Google+ for community management, consider tracking call volume, call handling time, time to resolution, and any other non-Google+ stats. The numbers that matter to you most should be out-of-system, but you can keep an eye on a few metrics while looking to grow your audience.

Value Your Audience

The asset most companies undervalue is the connection with other people. Sales professionals know that they are only as good as their email address book (or Rolodex) (and then the ability to close), but in most other professions, the importance of building a network of any value is rarely directly measured or rewarded. And yet, that's where a great deal of your business value can be derived.

Referrals are gold. There's hardly a business that doesn't count referrals from past customers as the #1 source of new and valuable leads. Yet most companies overlook the importance of building a network and instead place emphasis on traditional advertising methods, hard-sell outbound marketing (in email and direct mail), and sales-only interactions (versus relationship-based marketing).

You need to build an audience that matters to your organization (no matter the size). I won't answer the question of who should be in your audience. You would know that better than me. Your audience should be composed of people related to a topic, region, wealth, or some other demographic that you know. It's hard to segment people on Google+ in those ways. (Although the third-party site findpeopleonplus.com certainly gives it a try.) It's up to you to put together and understand the dynamics of your audience.

You should also build an audience that's useful to your business goals. More important, you need to turn your audience into a community. You need to express to your audience that sustainable, relationship-minded business is important to you. If you seek strictly transaction-based selling, you won't get the results you expect.

Further, third-party applications do not help grow your audience on Google+. Agencies and other consulting groups might offer services to help with this kind of thing, but at this point, they are strictly manual, and the value of this type of service is suspect. Ask for a sense of the methodology used before choosing to accept anyone's offer of this nature.

Sales are important to business, as is marketing, especially referrals. However, treat your community in a way that makes these seem secondary to your mission. Engage your community, and we'll agree on the best way to treat your community.

What Interests Your Audience

If you treat your audience right, it will appreciate you and perhaps even become a community within which you participate before you ever ask for anything. That's the best possible outcome. But before discussing this further, let's talk about what I mean by "community."

I use the term "community" gently because most people tend to think of a community as a static thing with boundaries and numbers. They look at how many people "like" their Facebook page and think that's the number. They look at their email list and think that's the number. They see how many followers they have on Twitter and how many people have circled them on Google+ and think that's the number. However, community is a lot more fluid. It's actually only the active and lurking (but attentive) people who count as your community.

Following are some of the reasons people give for following other people:

- I follow people who have filled out a profile and have a picture. If they don't take the time to fill out a profile, why should I care about them?

- I follow people who get mentioned by other people I follow. If you're mentioned in a post and I check you out and you're interesting, I add you to a circle.

- I circle people if I'm interested in what they post.

- I look at people who leave interesting comments on other people's posts. If they can hold up their end of the conversation, I circle them.

- I want value. If you're not sharing something of value, I won't circle you.

- I want personal takes, not just your business thoughts.

- I want interesting and original, not just reshared information.

These responses reflect what many people consistently say. In short, people want many different things, and everyone is of a different mind about the criteria for selecting who they put in which circle.

These might seem like common sense, but many business professionals (especially those in larger companies) using Google+ often get more than two of these recommendations wrong. For instance, several company employees do not fill out their profiles, making it vague about where they work within an organization, and throw off warnings about whether to trust them. In other cases, I saw that two-way conversations weren't happening much for representatives of companies (including two different owners of smaller businesses), never commenting back on the questions and conversation starters that interested potential community members left on these people's posts.

Everything your audience is interested in matters.

What Community Means to People

When you ask people on Google+ about what they value in communities, the answers are far more consistent and focused than you would think. It's useful to think about this because growing an audience is one level of connection, but growing an engaged community is even more ideal. Aim for community if you value a relationship with your buyer that lasts beyond a simple transaction. If you simply have the "one and done" mentality, an audience can suit you. (Although I rarely hear anyone freely admit that they want only transactions and not relationships.)

A community, in the eyes of the people I spend time with on Google+, is a two-way medium. If you want to build a stronger audience, you must spend time commenting on your posts and on other people's posts. Several people indicated that you should take the time to talk back to people.

In the blogging world, you have to be the #1 commenter on your own blog. It's also true of Google+. We talk a bit more about commenting in a moment.

Bring a Campfire

Another important part of community is that you need to bring a "campfire." You need something for people to gather around to talk about. A campfire can be a shared interest, a common goal, or something collaborative.

In advising larger companies, I often point out that it's hard to build a "Sprite" community (no offense to that delicious lemon/lime beverage) because the people who drink Sprite don't have a lot of reasons to gather simply based on beverage choice.

Not all beverages are created equal. If you're Jones Soda, for instance, your campfire might be about the shared photos on the bottles. If you're Moxie soda, you might have a regional appeal. (I'm from Maine, and if you've never had a Moxie, it's this acquired taste that the majority of people who taste consider to be horrible, but many folks love and cherish.)

The campfire for car enthusiasts is obvious. I used to own a Saturn (five of them over a span of years), and the company did a lot to promote that folksy feeling. I now own a Camaro and their online communities (none of them run by GM) are full of passionate enthusiasts who talk with you endlessly about details that would make anyone's eyes glaze—even manufacturers. But that's the campfire.

So, if you want to attempt the community route, come up with a campfire. If you're a travel company, it's fairly easy. If you're a soap company, maybe your campfire is talking about the home spa movement, which doesn't exist, but you can launch it. If you're the UPS Store franchisee, maybe your campfire is the local small business community angle for your region.

Connecting People Is Key

Communities where people spend their time are those that help them connect to other people who share their interests. I wrote about this in *Trust Agents*, saying that a trust agent works to "be the elbow of every deal." You can do the same thing on Google+.

If you're the person who points out the interesting people that share great things, you can have a growing following. The more you can share connections and contacts without asking for reciprocity, the more likely you'll be in positions that can later prove useful.

This is something most people do naturally (and well) offline. If you play golf, for example, you know that it's the conversation over that course that makes the day wonderful. The game itself is the campfire. But business people don't just play golf for the love of the game. They use that time to build and strengthen relationships and to share contacts to seed future business.

The same is just as true online. It's sometimes difficult to master the nuances, but observe others, and you can gain a sense of it. This chapter has plenty of the nuances you should explore. Connecting people is a vital part of the game.

The Time in Between Is Important

Another element of growing your audience is continuity. People want to hear from you (or the leaders of your community) on a fairly regular basis. They want a sense of their online "place" being familiar and "known."

In these busy times, many of us cannot gather face to face as often as we would like. We travel for business. We scratch out time to be with our families. We work on our own pursuits. So, getting together as often as we'd like falls fairly far down on the priority list. After the financial downturn of 2009–2011, many companies forcibly cut back business travel, which is a perfect reason to build stronger online communities.

Continuity enables conversations you've had in person to continue online. Using tools such as Hangouts you can invite other parts of the company into the conversation. You can gather neighborhood businesses for a quick mid-day meeting without requiring anyone to leave the stores. This need to keep a "place" alive in between meetings works for all sizes of businesses.

Familiarity and continuity help people feel connected in between those isolated events. For instance, if you make gourmet cookies, and you decide to build your community around the campfire of "gift basket design," you might share videos from your in-store seminars and then invite others in both your offline and your online community to participate in posts you put up related to this. It's a way to move the online and offline conversations into a continuum that can prove useful for that sense of sustained contact.

You Are a Media Company

Communities want content, which isn't too far afield of the campfire premise. However, in this case, the audience you build wants unique information consistently posted. They want information, stories, videos, ideas, and conversations about the campfire that holds your community together.

Building an audience requires a rather consistent stream of this. Most of the examples in previous chapters suggest posting two to four times a day on average. It also means commenting on other people's posts, sharing other people's posts (but not as often as you create your own), and connecting with the people you build relationships with online.

This takes time. It can take up to an hour a day (perhaps broken into two 30-minute slots). Some people and companies devote even more than that per day. Try different tactics and investments in time and measure the results (how many people click through, how many comments, how many +1's, or any other in-system metrics) to see what is effective.

Make Your Buyer the Hero

People in your community want concepts they can adapt for their own use. They want ideas that improve their own world. "Make your buyer the hero," is a phrase I use quite often that applies here. Concepts and tactics (or recipes or something similar) are what people want from you.

I started blogging in 1998. It took 8 years to get 100 readers. The reason was that Really Simple Syndication (RSS) wasn't invented and blogs weren't popular. (We called them "journals.") However, the reality I stress with new bloggers is that I hadn't yet learned to write for my readers.

It's the same in your efforts to build an audience. If you write about yourself and your products and how great you are, only you can benefit from that. If you create interesting posts with concepts and ideas for your community to take so that they can improve their own experience in life, you have something.

Sailing the High C's of Audience Building

It all comes down to the letter C:

- **Community:** It takes precedence above audience.
- **Campfire:** It's something to gather around.
- **Connections:** Create them between members of your community and share your network.

- **Continuity:** Keep things consistent; blend the offline and online worlds.

- **Content:** Make your posts interesting.

- **Concepts:** Educate others and empower them.

With this as a method for growing your audience, go forth and start experimenting. Learn what you can do to grow your community. Send a letter to your email list inviting them to connect with you on Google+. Encourage your offline customer base to connect with you there as well. Make it easy for people to navigate to your presence on Google+. And build with all the tools we've shared.

12

Sharing

The ability to share other people's posts and information on Google+ is something that the Google team stated as one of the major reasons why it built the platform, and it shows. The blue link to share a post is directly listed at the bottom of every post (see Figure 12-1)—except those where the creator of the post disables sharing. So, within the system, it's easy to share other people's interesting finds.

Figure 12-1 The share link in Google+.

Bringing information into Google+ from the outside is also helpful; sharing other people's ideas interspersed with your own shows your audience members that you care about their education and entertainment as much as you care about getting the sale. (And yes, you need to entertain your audience.) Whether posting or sharing information from people's blogs that you find useful, or sharing links to articles that relate to your business or your location, sharing information is a great way to build audience, to round out people's perceptions of you and your business, and an opportunity to connect others with useful information that keeps them coming back to you for more interesting finds.

This chapter discusses the value of the content you share and what you should be sharing.

The Value of Content Curation

Steve Rosenbaum has been championing content curation for all the years that I've known him. His book, *Curation Nation*, is an excellent source of ideas on how to do sharing the right way, and it makes a great complement to this chapter. Steve is the CEO of Magnify.net, a site that helps you collect and organize video content into useful groupings.

Sharing is just as important (maybe more) as creating original and unique content. People want to follow your interests, not just your company updates. A great strategy for sharing is one that helps you gain a following for what you share but also rounds out people's perspectives on what you believe in and what you (and your organization) are about.

Steve says this:

"Sharing used to be a 'nice' thing to do. But that was back when other ways of finding things worked. Media used to work. Search used to work. But today, all the old systems that filtered out noise and created context are broken. So sharing becomes the only thing we can trust to separate signal from noise.

When Chris Brogan tells me to pay attention to Google+, I do so because I know he's been into this whole social media thing for a very long time and he's been right before. If he points me to articles, posts, sites, or people, I pay attention.

Sharing is more than just a pointer or a map: It's an implicit endorsement. So, by sharing things that matter, you are building your collective digital 'story', a story of what you believe in and what you endorse.

I call it digital clothing. When you wake up in the morning, you look in your closet and say, 'Today, I'll wear the blue shirt with the white collar.' You put on the image you want to share with the world. Increasingly, we live our lives online, so the links we share and the collection of information we curate and endorse becomes a critical part of who we are.

Put another way: We are what we share. And our friends and followers increasingly count on us to create a consistent digital identity and both create and share content that re-enforces that identity.

In a world of too much information, you can see how apps like FlipBoard take our social network, overlay it with what the people we value are endorsing, and create an editorial experience that is shockingly interesting. It is what Sci-Fi writers have been promising for a long time, a daily newspaper that is essentially 'The Daily Me.' Only, it's better. It's 'The Daily Us.'"

Just when I think I know Steve's perspective, he comes up with a term like "digital clothing." Now, I'd probably think of it more as "accessories," but either way, he's right. "Clothes make the man," is the old expression, and what Steve is saying is that people check out what you "wear" by checking out what you "share."

Further, his premise, *The Daily Us*, is a great way to look at it. If you're a real estate professional, for instance, this is a great way to show community. Imagine gathering up the go-to information on your neighborhood and putting it in a digital newspaper (such as Google+) for others to find.

Your locals, the people you count on for referrals, will come to this shared information, your own version of *The Daily Us*, and they'll see themselves in the paper, and other information that's useful to them. But even better for you, this paper, complete with all kinds of keywords about the area, can be searched for and found by your potential prospects, those moving to the area. Do you see how this can be useful?

A little later in this chapter, you learn about the mindset of building a magazine. Keep what Steve said in mind when you get there. But first, meet someone who shares simply because it spreads good feelings.

Sharing as a Practice

I asked Mahei Foliaki, who identifies himself as a Chief Happiness Officer, Google+ Tipster, and Ideas Engineer, what he knows about sharing and why he shares what he does. I've known Mahei from Twitter since somewhere around 2008, I believe, where he goes by @iconic88. On every platform where I've seen him, Mahei is about sharing. On Twitter, you have only 140 characters, so Mahei's shares are mostly just repointing us to good information.

On Google+, he gets the chance to explain what's interesting, to sum up the content he's read, and to make his contributions to the stream on Google+ valuable. I have found what Mahei shares to be of value to my business and my life overall. (Oh, and beyond that, he's just a friendly connector type.)

Mahei said the following:

> "Sharing is caring. I have an absolute focus on making our world a better place because that is the way I was raised. Making a difference and all that super positive 'goose-bumpy,' 'behind the neck, hair-raising, and wow! that's helpful' stuff. My sharing is simply about empowering and inspiring my friends, my networks, and my new connections, who over time, eventually become friends, to making their world a little easier and happier. I am very fortunate that my parents and other wise family members instilled in me a long time ago to be of service and to be the example that we want our world to be.
>
> We have an expression from back home in Tonga, which is a small Pacific Island nation nestled deep in the South Pacific next to Fiji: 'Ko Tonga Mo'unga ki He Loto' translated means 'The Mountain of Tonga is within you.' Us Tongan people don't own many material things compared to other economically wealthier societies but what we do have is our love for others. This is the raw essence of why I share what I share because I know it will help someone. Any form of gratitude is a reflection of the rich values that have been passed down to me from my parents, my family, my ancestors, my culture, and Pacific peoples.

Advice: Share to help, inspire, and empower. Be consistent and people will eventually know you for what you share and how you have been helpful to them. You won't please everyone because we all value different things. It's all love any way and regardless of the content, people will remember your generosity of sharing a solution or eight."

What's great about Mahei is that he doesn't need anything from anyone. He chooses to share because he feels it's goodwill. We don't all have to emulate the Tongan mindset 100%, but bringing some of what Mahei's people do into how you conduct your business can result in goodwill that translates into better business relationships. It makes you a go-to person, or a connector, and that's useful.

Sharing becomes a "coin of the realm" in some ways because when you find good information for your following, and in sharing it, you get a little more of their attention. It's a transaction that builds interest (in both uses of the word).

Building Interest

With sharing, there's an opportunity to keep your audience interested by connecting with items of value. (Both from those things you've found within Google+, but also from finding information outside of the platform that can prove useful.) There are two ways to consider using this information: to stay on-topic and try to build more useful content for your community, or to go off-topic and let people see more about you than normal. Both build interest. In one case, you show someone that you have information that can help them grow in their pursuits and that you support that community. In the other case, you show that you're more than just what you post for work purposes. For instance, Jennifer Cisney often posts about dogs. You can't connect with her on Google+ and not know that she loves pugs (and dogs in general).

Should you do one and not the other? This doesn't have to be a decision about one or the other. You should consider doing both. But what if you have multiple interests? You decide what you want to share. You can share more than one side of you. One way to think about sharing is to consider yourself as a magazine publisher.

You Are a Magazine Publisher

Magazines rarely work as a potpourri collection of whatever comes to mind. Google+, maybe more than other social networking platforms, seems to value a somewhat consistent selection of topics for a user to share. For instance, if you share about jazz, photography, and your business subject, that's probably fine. If you also share about dogs, barbecue, interesting quotes, and vintage hammocks, you might have a trickier time. People won't understand the content focus of your "magazine," if this is how you curate.

This line of thinking might actually help you design your sharing strategy to overlay with your posting methodology. If you run a company that sells outboard motors for boats, you might post one or two posts a day about your products or your customers using your products. You might share a piece about great destinations for boating, a piece about innovative barbecue gadgets, and a piece about easy-but-exciting cocktail recipes because these things would be in alignment with your brand.

If you see the previous suggestions as a magazine, all those pieces would fit together, right? An article about Notre Dame football coaching changes would be a bit more afield of the primary buyer.

The recipe to find great stuff to share is split between filling your magazine with interesting material that connects with your "readers" but such that you also show off a bit of who you are outside of that editorial funnel. It's a balance. You should probably split on-topic and off-topic about 80/20, depending on the nature of your business and your position in the organization. If you work for customer service in a huge company, your personal life would likely be just as interesting as your perspective on the company's top buyers. If you're the CEO or president of a smaller company, stick closer to the magazine perspective.

Don't however let this analogy limit you. Instead, let it guide you. The more you think of yourself as building a magazine each time you post and share into your Google+ stream, those constraints of the analogy might actually help you make decisions about what works for you and your community. If for any reason this feels a bit restrictive, try it a different way.

Commenting on What You Share

Previous chapters talk about leaving comments, which are the life's blood of what builds business relationships on Google+. For sharing, you have an added benefit. Comments become the "liner notes" to what you're interested in, and they give you another way to add some context for your readers and audience.

Commenting gives your audience a chance to interact with you around the campfire. It allows people to share their opinions, and it gives people a sense of how you'll react when they bring their thoughts back to you. You need to comment back on as many posts as you can. The more you communicate in both directions with your audience, the better.

This one aspect of social networking and social media is the huge difference between business communications in the past and what can be accomplished today.

Similarly, in the past, magazines had a static "letters" column, whereas you can now talk with the authors and the editors of most magazines online at your whim. I write for *Entrepreneur* magazine and many times have had conversations with people who read my articles. In both perspectives (business and publishing), this ability to communicate via comments is a powerful boost to how your audience can interact with you, and how you're perceived. Take advantage of it.

What Does Your Magazine Look Like?

When asking people on Google+ what their show or magazine would look like, the answers were quite varied. One said his show would be like the *Jon Stewart* show (politics meets comedy). Another wants to be the "Gordon Ramsey of small business marketing." One friend wants to do a show called *Investing in Your Future Self*, about how you can grow and prosper.

The thing is, you can do whatever show you want. The platform exists. On Google+, you can upload YouTube videos, host live Hangouts, and start conversations around a picture, a post, or a reshare. It *is* your show. It *is* your magazine. Make something that draws attention, that grows an audience, that builds potential relationships, and that can convert to a prospective audience. It simply takes thought, time, and effort.

Create a magazine that gives you a framework to think about what resembles what the experience might feel like. There's a difference between the magazines you read and what you can create. Most magazines have more than one person putting them together. In this case, you're a one-person show, and to that point, you need some help with tools to build out your magazine. Curating interesting content is a great concept, but how can you accomplish this goal?

Two Resources to Help with Your Sharing

Does it take a lot of time to find interesting items to share? Not if you have some kind of a system in place. You can use another Google product to help find interesting things to share: Google Reader.

If you go to http://google.com/reader, you can find a tool that enables you to read multiple blogs and online magazines in an orderly fashion. What's great about Reader is that you can organize and share thousands of blogs and feeds based on your interests. If you use list mode, you see only headlines and a slender amount of detail from which you can decide to drill down and make even more sense of whichever articles catch your fancy.

Oh, but your reader starts out fairly empty. Where would you start looking for sites to add to it? Start at http://alltop.com, Guy Kawasaki's "magazine rack for the

Internet." You can find hundreds and hundreds of topic categories, under which there are hundreds and hundreds of blogs. It's a great way to start figuring out where to source material for your sharing needs. (Guy and I are friends, but I have no business interest in Alltop. It's just the right tool for this job.)

Find a few dozen (or if you're daring, a few hundred) blogs to skim through each day; read a few posts that you find interesting and that help you build up interesting content; then share that content into your Google+ by posting your thoughts and then a link to the original post. You'll give people something of value to consider.

To round this out a bit more, *now* consider creating a bit of a workflow. Google Reader and its place in this flow are mentioned shortly.

A Sharing Workflow

If you're not sure how to fit sharing into your other social networking tasks and time management for Google+, this section should help. You need to experiment, of course. Results can vary depending on what type of business you run, on whether your buyers have found their way onto Google+ yet, and a whole host of other variables.

A simple workflow might look something like this:

- Read other people's posts and comment where appropriate (10 minutes).

- Check previous posts of yours and comment back where appropriate (5–10 minutes).

- Find interesting information inside and outside of Google+ to share with your community (15–20 minutes).

- Share one or two posts (5 minutes).

- Create a unique post (10–30 minutes).

- Comment back and forth on posts (15–20 minutes).

This adds up. Social networking for business takes approximately 2 hours a day. The previous list addresses only Google+. If you add in practices such as blogging, using other social networks such as Facebook and Twitter, and other tasks, you can eat up significant time. The challenge is to understand what works and what doesn't, and tune your use of time so that you work for results and you're not just churning the waters all the time.

Time-wise, sharing is something that might take you between 15 to 20 minutes tops to get through, after you have a bit of a system. Go to Google Reader, look through topics that would fit with your "magazine," share one or two posts in the earlier part of the day, and maybe another one or two in the later part of the day.

Quick point to make: There isn't a specific or magic time to post information because it varies depending on your audience, on whether you're location-specific, on how people use social networks, and other factors. It's up to you to measure. Use Google Analytics. Use whatever other tools you have, but definitely measure and decide what you'll do.

Consider posting information at a few set times throughout the day: early in the morning to hit Europe and the east coast of the United States before people become too busy. Consider posting again around 2 p.m. Eastern time, which is right before lunch on the west coast of the United States. Then you can post around 7 p.m. Eastern time, which is when some folks are home, when the west coast people are getting ready to call it a day at the office, and when some Australians and New Zealanders start getting active. In this way, you can hit your worldwide demographic.

Experiment. You'll find what works.

Can Sharing Add Direct Business Value?

Depending on your company, sharing can certainly help to add business value. The question some people might need to answer is whether that can be directly tied back to your efforts on Google+. That answer is more difficult when it comes to sharing. It might be traceable when you post something original, and there's a call-to-action link or phone number embedded in the post. That certainly is measurable.

It's more difficult to measure whether sharing gives you a direct business value. A lot of actions you take as businesses (and in your lives) aren't easily measurable, and these change how you are perceived and "sweeten" the deal in your relationships. Sharing falls into this category.

13

Power Plays in Google+

This chapter discusses some of the best moves for business professionals to build relationships and drive forward some of their interests and efforts. It's still the early days with this platform, but the goal of this book is to talk about the mindset behind the use of Google+ more than the specific buttons you need to push to access the technology.

Google+ has power plays that can help you get a leg up in these early days. Heck, just being on Google+ means that you're ahead of the game. This chapter looks at the ideas of people who do interesting projects on Google+. Some of these ideas might be applicable to what you do with Google+ for your business.

John Herman: The Hangout Entertainer

I've known and admired John Herman as an artist and creator since 2007. I met him through Steve Garfield when he was in and around the PodCamp scene, like a lot of the people I know. John uses Google+ to create live video hangouts about all kinds of topics, including game shows, creative jams, and more.

Following is a recent example from John:

> **"Join me tonight in a zany Google+ Hangout:** Can you draw, dance, juggle, or sing? What else can you do? I will be in +Matthew Carano's hangout tonight at 8:30 p.m. ET for the *Google+ Hangouts Talent Show.* It is a blast! Past winners of the *GOLDEN GUITAR PIC* have included a Theremin performer from New Hampshire and a balladeer from Wisconsin. Winners also get an original song composed and performed *about* them.

> Please note: If you join, then you may be expected to perform for approximately two minutes. Others are selected as judges. I am hosting. I'll be the one in the tuxedo. See you tonight!"

Following is another example from John:

> **"TONIGHT: Who wants to hangout surf with me (and win a bow tie)?** In honor of National Bow Tie Day (yesterday), *Smith Brand Bow Ties* of San Francisco is providing tonight's *Google+ Hangouts Game Show* winner with a custom made bow tie by +Ian Smith himself. We are playing sometime after 8 p.m. (hint, hint). The first nine to jump into the hangout compete for the bow tie by answering trivia questions and completing physical challenges. I'll be hosting in a tuxedo. After the game show, I am jumping right over to +Matthew Carano's Cover of the Week hangout, where he will be teaching *In the Aeroplane over the Sea by Neutral Milk Hotel.* Double fun!"

Notice how John actually has sponsors already. In a month of doing Hangouts, which by their nature can host only around eight people live, John draws enough attention to get prize sponsors for his events. The power move is realizing that people appreciate entertainment and that you can use Google+ as a channel to entertain your prospects and partners through the use of Hangouts, video, text, photos, and even just commenting on posts.

If you sell a not-exactly-interesting product, what kind of "show" could you develop to make it more interesting to get that product in front of other people? Or who else is hosting an interesting show that you can find a way to partner with to distribute your products as gifts? There are many ways to think about this one, obviously, but why not start with such a creative idea? Be a huge fan of "why not?" as a business decision-parsing question.

Michael Dell: The Wide Open CEO

I've written about Michael Dell quite a few times in this book. Michael is perhaps the most active large-company CEO who has embraced Google+, so he is an interesting example. Michael uses Google+ in many ways, including bringing the company's storyline directly to the people. He's active in pointing out corporate news day in and day out, which isn't typically my recommendation, but in Michael's case, he gets a "pass" because he's so passionate. Dell *is* his life, or a significant part of it.

The power moves you can learn from Michael Dell are twofold: He uses Hangouts and uses conversations in and around his corporate news.

In a recent Hangout, Michael Dell lured Google co-founder Sergey Brin into a conversation. Imagine the power of this for a moment. If you're at all interested in business and technology, you suddenly have live video access to two huge company leaders, and you can ask whatever questions you want. (They might not answer, but the opportunity to seek a response from a top CEO is there.) In other Hangouts, Michael has answered questions about his position relative to HP's news about potentially moving out of the personal computing world.

There's a power to Michael Dell using video as well as text. On one level, when he's writing in text, there's a little worry that you're not getting the real Michael but a functionary or PR professional. (I believe that it's Michael himself, but not everyone feels that or believes that. It just is.) When there's just text, and when you know so many entertainment professionals outsource their keyboard efforts to other people, the perception is given. Because of that, you get an even bigger kick out of seeing Michael Dell just answering business questions live in video.

You might not (yet) be as big as Michael Dell or Sergey Brin. That's not the big point. The big opportunity for a power move here is that you can be accessible as a business leader and that matters. Is there a huge return on investment to putting yourself in front of the community? It might be hard to trace it to a number on a spreadsheet, but you'd be hard pressed to find a PR agency that wouldn't advocate for this.

Muhammad Yunus: Changing the World

Reading Professor Muhammad Yunus's job occupation as it's listed on Google+ might give you pause: "Creating a world without poverty." That's what occupies him. As the founder of the Grameen Bank, Professor Yunus spends a good deal of time showing through example how his work in teaching people how to lend money to the poor rural citizens of Bangladesh (as of May 2011, Grameen Bank has 8.4 million borrowers, 97% of which are women, with a nearly 100% payback rate) might help others change the world.

None of this has anything to do with Google+. Professor Yunus did this work the old-fashioned way: in person, on huge stages, and with handshakes from world leaders all over the world. But what has come back to Google+ is a new and powerful stage from which Professor Yunus can share his travels, his efforts, and the ongoing story of the work of empowering the poor to build better lives. If you read his posts, each one is a blend of education and an opportunity for others to participate in some way (not even necessarily his own projects, but ideas that seed other projects).

By sharing his day-to-day life in pictures, text, and videos, Professor Yunus shows that these victories are made up of several components. That's the power move. If you're working on slow-moving projects, on projects that maybe don't always draw the sustained attention of the mainstream, Google+ becomes a media center where you can build information that others will opt into and find inspiring. Instead of simply sharing this information on his website, Professor Yunus brings this out to the outpost where everyone can read a stream of interesting posts from others so that people can remember to think of the larger story in the frenzy of their days.

Mark Horvath: Handing Out Pizza, Socks, and Hope

I've known Mark Horvath, founder of InvisiblePeople.tv and WeAreVisible.com, since 2008. We met in the hallways of Gnomedex, after I saw his presentation about how he films the stories of everyday homeless people to give them a voice and a face, and how he gives socks, pizza slices, and whatever else he can get his hands on to the homeless wherever he goes. Mark happens to be the only person working full time on Invisible People, so he's part president, part secretary, part worker bee, and part cameraman. Here's his take.

Mark has brought a lot of attention to the homeless through his videos, and he has brought attention to the project by being active on Twitter as @hardlynormal. (If you're a Twitter user, go follow him now.) He's brought this to Google+, where he can clearly and simply show the videos. The beauty of Mark's platform on Google+ is that he can now open up to conversations. You can leave comments on YouTube, but the general quality of comments on that platform isn't necessarily all that useful. Again, like Professor Muhammad Yunus, Mark can now slot his stories about the homeless into the stream we're participating in already.

What you can learn from Mark is that telling a story is always more impactful than simply asking for something. Secondly, you can learn that simple small bites are just as important as the big bites. Professor Yunus works on a larger scale changing the world, and Mark puts socks in the hands of people who need them. Do we argue about which is more important to the poor person who needs help in the moment? We don't. We need Mark every bit as much as we need Muhammad Yunus. That both gentlemen are bringing their passionate work to Google+ where we can interact with it shows you how they value the platform.

I asked Mark Horvath what he thought about Google+ as a channel. His response might be something you feel when thinking about whether Google+ is the place for you.

> "Google+ started. I had not yet jumped into the pond because they had yet to make it available for people with Google Apps accounts (as an NPO, Google allows me to use its Apps service free). My primary email address runs on its servers. That's the account I want to use, but it has not yet invited Google Apps users to Google+ yet, and I just didn't want to have a new place that 'sucks' my time away. As someone with AAADHD (I have a triple A personality), anything 'new' is a distraction. I saw the obvious potential but was scared that once I stuck my toe in the water, I'd have to jump into the pond.
>
> About a month ago I logged in and noticed someone had posted one of the InvisiblePeople.tv videos, and it had 48 comments. That's huge! For what I do, the conversation is gold. The videos are only the catalyst to start the conversations.
>
> It's only through interactive communication that InvisiblePeople.tv is able to shift paradigms to help save lives by ending homelessness. Really the end goal of InvisiblePeople.tv is to fix a broken system by empowering homeless people to tell their own stories. Homeless services rarely listen to the people we serve. Brands would be out of business if they didn't listen to their customers. In contrast, not one homeless person has suggested, 'Throw me in a room with 100 other men, giving us mats to sleep on the floor and one bathroom to share. Then, kick me out every day at 5 a.m., even in the winter. That will heal my mental illness and drug addiction!' Yet, that's exactly what we have done for the last 100 years. We have warehoused homeless people.
>
> Anyway, without going into all that, InvisiblePeople.tv's main purpose is to change the system to save lives and taxpayer dollars. It works. Housing programs have started. Countries, state governments, cities, and NPOs have even invited me to travel and help them find solutions.
>
> So, I did start adding new videos to Google+, but I wasn't spending much time there. Now, thanks to you giving me a kick in the butt, I have to just jump right into a new media channel. But we make time for what's important, and the conversation on Google+ is very important."

Mark's point, that this is yet another technology channel, that this is yet another place to have to distribute media and then respond, is valid. We are all overtaxed. There are too many things on our lists already. And yet, people are taking action and spending time learning how these tools can help them.

Robert Scoble and Rackspace

Robert Scoble is a long-time tech visionary and media maker, with a lengthy career as someone always out there looking for game-changing, bleeding-edge items of note. He's thoroughly passionate about finding out how interesting technology can change people's worlds for the better. He currently works with Rackspace, a technology company out of Texas.

Following are Robert's thoughts about what's going on to change the game inside of Google+:

> "Social enterprises move and respond to customers and partners in real time. Google+ enables that. How? You can see a customer request coming through your feed. You can start a video hangout with that customer, or team of customers. Then you can get your co-workers in another circle where they can help you answer questions in real time and you can go at it.

> What are Rackspace's Google+ power moves?
> - Building circles of industry thought leaders that can inform my daily conversation. I have 5,000 people inbound separated into circles of investors, journalists, analysts, other social media representatives, executives, entrepreneurs, and co-workers.
>
> - Working on setting up a reciprocal system. I help them by +1'ing their posts, commenting on them, sharing their best posts, telling my audience to follow them, and so on.
>
> - Developing a story. In Rackspace's case, our story that we want the world to know is 'those folks are up to date on the latest cloud technology and they have the best support.' So, how do we develop that story? At Red Bull, the story will be one of extreme sports. Every brand will have a different story, and it needs to be developed over time with every post, every photo, every video.

> All of this is aimed at driving relationships that bring us thought leadership points, but also that turn into real business."

Robert has demonstrated a lot of different ways to use his influence to learn, to find stories that tell the larger story of his business, and to build an actionable community, instead of simply following people willy-nilly without a plan. In his power plays are all kinds of ways for you to consider how your own business might implement some of these ideas.

My Power Plays

In summing this up, I want to share some of what I've been experimenting with over the last several months so that you might consider which of these are useful to your business. I often experiment with several ideas and angles so that I can report back on what I discover, but you wouldn't want to mimic all that I'm doing because I'm making steps forward and backward to see what results I can observe from those experiences. Therefore, some of what I do has a negative impact. Plan accordingly. Following is a list of my moves:

- To get more people to add you to circles: If you want a somewhat broad and untargeted following on Google+, the best way to get people to circle you is to find information from outside of Google+ (versus resharing what's going around) that is at once interesting, entertaining, and useful. The more times you do that, the more the number of people who circle you will jump.

- To get more people to add you to circles, fill out your profile in detail, but not overly so (a few paragraphs will suffice). Use the links. Make it easy for people to contact you.

- To get more people to engage with you, comment much more often on other people's posts. Circle 100 or so people you think are interesting, important, or helpful, and comment frequently on their material with something thoughtful (or sometimes funny) to say.

- To have people click your links more often, provide interesting context before the link, and try to make the links not be simply promotional for your own business. The most action people take on links I post in Google+ are when I've written the information before the link such that the person realizes that what I'm offering will be helpful to *them*. This is the magic formula.

- Posting too much waters down people's responses to you. Posting too rarely means that your information flows past in the stream and gets lots. I'm not yet sure the perfect posting timing or volume (if there even is such a thing), but an abundance of posts means a shortcoming in clicks or comments, and that posting a few thoughtful pieces (maybe no more than four a day) amounts to more activity all the way around.

- To mix Google+ into your business overall, think of it as part community engagement platform, part media sharing environment, part customer service handling, and part sales lead generation. Of these, I try to do those four items in that order of importance. You would think customer service comes first, but community is about more than the people who have issues.

- If you want your information to travel far, always post it to public and not to a limited group of circles. The more hoops you make people jump through to circle, the shorter the distance of the shares.

Your mileage may vary. In thinking through what kinds of power plays might be useful to you as a business, you might also want to see more about "How do I convert sales?" The thing is, that's what I've been teaching for this entire book, only I've been showing you the variation of "subtle" and "relationship-minded" versus hard and down marketing. Let's talk about that a bit more.

In coming to an understanding about how Google+ can help grow your business, the power plays in this chapter focus on those uses of Google+ that highlight a way to help buyers and prospects get a better connection to you and your company. The main reasoning behind this is that you buy from people you like. You buy from people you know. Using these tools enables people to get the sense that they know you and understand you a bit more. This is a way to introduce yourself to someone before you actually meet them.

To work through how these kinds of moves might work for your business is to accept that you feel your business is interested in your customers, and that you feel relationships ahead of sales can lead to a more loyal customer, who might offer repeat business at best, and barring that, might at least become the best source of referrals to you. This is the gold standard of how engaging in social networks such as Google+ can work for you. If you build relationships, these build the opportunity for more opt-in conversations, which build the chance to sell to people who feel they have an affinity for you, and which ultimately leads to customers who then offer better referrals than those who purchased in a more transactional manner.

As with all things, every one of these power plays take time. They're not built for quick-and-fast ways to get the most from Google+ and make millions tomorrow. I'm sure someone will post that book. I'm sure ebooks are out there that seek to sell you on super-fast ways to make millions with social networks such as Google+. I've never seen those tactics work. Instead, taking some time and building meaningful contact with people is always in style and always brings some level of response.

Are social networks for everyone? Not necessarily. I had breakfast recently at Rolly's Diner in Auburn, Maine. I sat beside a guy who did roofing for a living. In the space of my meal, he had three different people approach him for an estimate for a job. Three prospects found this man sitting beside me at the counter at a diner and asked him to help them with their needs. I said to him that it's obvious his work is quality, based on all those referrals, and I asked him whether he advertised in any formal way. "I'm here for breakfast and supper almost every day. That's all the advertising I do."

On the other side of the equation, people are learning that the physical world isn't always the best way to get your business to grow. Dane Cook, the comedian, visited Google headquarters for a chat with Google employees, and during that visit, he mentioned that what drove him to use MySpace (then Twitter, now Google+) to build community and share his work, and ultimately become one of the biggest names in comedy currently performing, was the realization that the other way to do it was to wait all week for that sliver of time in the middle of the night at that one comedy club, where only a few dozen people might be watching. By using social networks, he had the power to create comedy wherever and whenever he wanted, and build community by letting people anywhere in the world watch it wherever and whenever they wanted.

To me, the power of these power plays is that it gives you the chance to use Google+ as an outpost with a stage, and that you might now build the perfect blend of informative, entertaining, and useful information to drive value for prospects, buyers, and those you hope to encourage for a referral. In reviewing these moves, please seek to tie them to your larger business strategies because you want them to match with the rest of your goals and objectives. Social networking and social business performed out on an iceberg isn't useful to the larger business. You can experiment away from the main business for a while, but ultimately, you want your goals and strategies to all be in alignment with the business as a whole.

14

Setting Up Your Business Page

The strangest part of talking with people about writing a book was that they often said, "How can you write a book about Google+ for business if they haven't even released the business pages yet?" That was the case when I started the book. Business pages hadn't been launched. But I felt then the same way I feel now: Business pages are useful, but they are not central to how one conducts business on Google+. In their early days, many people weren't all that happy with the lack of features.

The Look and Feel of the Business Pages

A Google+ business page looks similar to a user profile page with a few exceptions for how the pages act and what's involved with them. They have a space for a brand avatar (this seems to be the default for branded pages at this point; although, I tend to recommend brands that promote with human faces), an area at the top for five pictures, and an area for posts.

There is a button to +1 the business page and a button to share the business page to your own circles. There is also a way to connect your Google+ business page with your primary website via the +1 functionality. Further down, you also see a button to create your own page should that appeal to you. There is likely to be more functionality added to that area of the page, over time.

At the time of launch, business pages enable only one administrator. This will no doubt change in future versions because leaving a single point-of-failure like that won't be advisable. This administrator is listed on the brand page so that people understand who has claimed ownership of the page. Business pages don't (yet) show authorship, so any post made by the business page will be marked as having been posted by the business page's title and not an individual person's name.

Several rules in place are helpful to the Google+ community at large insofar as feeling comfortable with the actions and activities of a brand on this social network. Many of these rules have been made with the individual user in mind and do not favor the business. That is a selling point, I'm sure, for more business activity to take place on Google+ because users will understand that their best interests are kept in mind by Google in this implementation.

Rules for Business Pages

Let's look at some of the rules of the business pages. A business page can't add people to circles until the individuals have circled that business page. Thus, if I'm representing Coca Cola, I can't go and circle Glenda Watson Hyatt and send her updates until Glenda circles me first. If you like Coke, circle Coke. If you don't want updates from that brand, don't circle it. You'll barely know they are around if you don't circle them.

Brand pages can't circle other brand pages. At the time of launch, if I'm Kodak, I can't circle Dell. This might change as time goes on because perhaps if I'm someone like Dell, I'd want Latitude to have a page, Inspiron to have a page, and for Dell to circle those two pages to keep track of all the larger brands. At launch, however, this isn't an option.

You as a user can circle whoever you want, so you can circle all the brands and businesses and organizations that you find useful. We'll talk about that more later. I just want to make the distinction between you the user and you the administrator of the business page.

Brand page users can't join other people's hangouts, but they can host hangouts. Thus, if you and your friends are hosting a "camera talk hangout," Kodak can't join that hangout via their brand page. However, if Kodak wants to host a hangout, users can join its hangout (if invited). Business pages can't yet join mobile hangouts, either.

Beyond this, some other features and details of brand pages are worth talking about.

A verification system is in the works at present. At the time I was writing this, it was still a bit "Wild West" how brands verified their accounts, and a few challenges had already arisen from enthusiasts rushing in to build brand pages for businesses and products and services they liked. This will naturally require some further consideration, and a process will be implemented to make this a lot simpler, and a lot less human-heavy, as most Google processes are automated.

Coming Soon (or Already Here)

A few features that didn't come out in the initial rollout bear discussing because they will come out soon and might be out by the time you read this book. The danger in writing about what isn't yet there is that it will change. But as the majority of this book isn't a log of features and services, I hope you'll forgive any changes.

Google is working on Places integration for brands that have physical locations, such as Starbucks or McDonald's. Places integration will give businesses the ability to post more details about specific locations, such as hours of operation, reviews, and more. I believe this will be a powerful addition to business pages on Google+, especially for smaller local businesses because it will help better integrate search and discovery.

Speaking of search, if you go to Google search (http://google.com) and put in the term "+nike" instead of "nike," Google now recognizes that + to mean that you'd like to find a branded business page on Google+ for Nike, and not Nike's primary website. Thus, if you want to connect with someone at Kodak on Google+, simply enter "+kodak" into Google search, and information would come up. This is new and a significant change to the Google search engine. It also speaks to how Google wants even more traffic to flow through its system, with the external goal being to help people find what they're seeking.

Another feature that business page administrators can expect soon is an integration to Google Analytics. If Google expects businesses to spend more time working and populating its Google+ business pages, it must deliver analytical value. This feature should be out in early 2013, if not sooner in some rudimentary form. I haven't seen how the analytics tie into your previous Google Analytics efforts, nor whether it will seamlessly track a user from Google+ to your site, and back again. Google will do everything it can to give administrators a great deal of data in this regard.

How Businesses Might Use These Pages

In thinking through how businesses might use Google+, I've placed emphasis on how people can connect and find other people of interest. Using the search tools inside Google+ and third-party services such as findpeopleonplus.com, you have many opportunities to seek out the kinds of people who might be potential buyers of your product. Following are a few ways to interact with people:

1. **As an education tool:** Use your business page on Google+ to give people information about your products and services to help them better determine whether a product is a fit for them. Imagine hosting live video hangouts a few times a week to answer questions about specific features that might have otherwise held someone back from buying.

2. **As a customer service channel:** Use your business page to help existing customers with issues. Field problem issues and get them resolved. Update the community as a whole of any larger problems or outages. Provide resolution videos and how-to information in video format to clear up frequently asked questions.

3. **As a community platform:** Make your customers a place to hang out and talk about the use of your products and services and other related products and services, such that you contribute to their success. If you sell health insurance, maybe that means a wellness-minded community. If you sell homes in Louisville, Kentucky, perhaps that means you keep the local calendar updated. You can make your platform successful in many ways.

4. **As a media center:** Create and share interesting videos and audio and ebooks and whatever other media. Source and curate the best of the user-generated media that represents your product and service. Build interesting content from other sources to augment the experience of people in your buying community. For instance, if you're the brand manager for the Ford Mustang, post YouTube videos that feature the

Mustang, but maybe also show off interesting videos from competitive muscle cars. (As a Camaro owner, I still watch videos about the Mustang and the Challenger, for instance.)

5. **As a collaboration space:** Imagine being Wacom and hosting artist meetups and hangouts. People could join the Wacom hangout to share techniques on how to do various interesting art forms. Imagine being Gibson guitars and hosting hangouts where you can see Gibson artists playing and then going into lessons and jams with other enthusiasts. There are some exciting ways to look at this. And don't let my examples fool you. Several business-to-business applications exist for building an enthusiastic collaboration space, too.

These are just five larger serving suggestions for how you might use the Google+ business page in some form that benefits the buying audience. In the early days of the launch, I saw most people using business pages as a kind of press release center. Though it's important that the community at large be briefed on new and upcoming situations, releases, and the like, I suspect that people on social networks won't seek out interactions with a business that speaks mostly through press releases.

Try imagining yourself at a cocktail party, where you represent your company. Walk up to that friendly-seeming guy, shake hands, and then talk about your incredible fourth-quarter stock earnings. Jarring, isn't it? Though a cocktail party isn't exactly the analogy of all social networks, it's reasonably useful in explaining the not-exactly-buttoned-up nature of users interacting via these platforms. Not everyone using a social network seeks a strictly business interaction, and as such, you might consider that with how you represent the voice of your company on your business page.

Interesting Business Pages of Note

In looking over how businesses and brands use their pages, I found a few for you to consider.

The Corcoran Group: https://plus.google.com/106654503918907830147/posts

This is a real estate company from New York City. I love that it has implemented a lot of ideas that I've written about before, including pointing out the interesting sights to see around New York. On the day I visited the company's page, it pointed out Rob Pruitt's statue of Andy Warhol, which I saw in person just the day before. It also shared a restaurant review and many more photos of scenic locations.

That alone would have been interesting enough for me, but I was excited to see that the Corcoran Group also hosted a few hangouts, chatting with people on video about real estate in New York, I'd imagine. What was interesting was that one of the hangouts was with another real estate company. I don't know whether they're competitors, but I'm excited to consider the possibility that businesses can share their best ideas via Google+ with noncompetitors.

The Dallas Cowboys: https://plus.google.com/ 106281600940449244340/posts

This is the official page of an NFL football team, and as such, several pictures of players are posted. Some of the photos are similar to the kind you'd expect in *Sports Illustrated*, and those are fine, but what interests me are the behind-the-scenes photos and the captured moments. For instance, there is a snap of Cowboys kicker David Buehler pretending to punch the mascot, Rowdy, after a game. In another photo, the Cowboys introduced one of the cheerleaders, Holly Arielle, who was a featured rookie of the week.

Most exciting to me were questions to fans of the team about various upcoming experiences. For instance, whoever runs the page asked people who from the Cowboys roster should be on the All-Pro team. This kind of engagement, when followed up by comments back to the various votes of the fans, is a great way to keep people feeling seen and heard.

Intel: https://plus.google.com/111660275132722215045/ posts

When writing about the technology of social media, it's often easiest to find examples of tech companies doing interesting things. What stood out immediately to me about the Intel business page was that it asks people who chose to circle the page to identify with which circle they wanted Intel to place them in: Technology Enthusiasts, Newsroom, or Life at Intel. This is brilliant.

Immediately, with this gesture, Intel has basically said, "We know that not everything we post will be for everyone. If you want to receive X kind of news, we'll add you to the X circle, and send you only that." This is smart and something to highlight and underline for your own potential implementation of a business page.

I also loved Intel's use of video on its page to tell stories. In one video, Intel features blogger Scott Schumann, the sartorialist. By using its products to tell stories about its users, and then creating well-produced video to share on its page, Intel engages while showing off the benefits of its products. This is a great move.

Edelman Digital: https://plus.google.com/ 106069281351191490929/posts

This is a PR agency, so I expected to see its page stuffed with client-related posts. I was pleasantly surprised to see more of a "life at Edelman" mixed with "things PR practitioners would find interesting" kind of mix. There was video, links to blog posts, photos of the team, and such.

If you want to talk about your company, it's interesting to talk to your peers in this way. I found the posts engaging enough to make me come back, even though I'm not in the market for Edelman's services. Instead, I appreciate what caught the page curator's attention, and I found surfing through the people they chose to circle to be worthwhile, too.

Finally, I like that Edelman uses the page as part of a hiring funnel. If you engage with the pages and find the people in the pictures interesting, you might want to learn more about working at Edelman Digital. It's an interesting way to share the flavor of the business and then encourage people to jump in.

Forbes: https://plus.google.com/ 116243183460563505245/posts

Several media properties are quite active in the business pages on Google+. In most cases, media companies post links to their articles. This is to be expected.

I like how *Forbes* and the other brand pages for media properties I visited highlight stories on its own site but provide enough of a fresh synopsis as to feel like they were curated and picked, instead of just foisted on us. If you want to follow a business publication, this is certainly one for your list. And I have hopes for the future of *Forbes* and the other media properties.

Forbes, like many others, has video in its arsenal. I'd like to see some of its video interviews peppered on this wall. *Forbes* also has quite a staff of writers, and it would be interesting if they all had Google+ accounts and came around to add to the conversations that happen when the magazine posts a story. I would love to see *Forbes* host hangouts with important business voices and invite in some of the audience to listen in. See how amazing this could be?

NASA: https://plus.google.com/ 103371865054310418159/posts

The folks who bring us rocket ships and space walks have an engaging brand presence on many social networks, but I feel they've found their stride with Google+. With fascinating videos and brilliant photographs, plus several astronauts and other

NASA employees hanging around to post updates and share comments, NASA has a great opportunity here.

Schools can benefit from arranging live hangouts with their classrooms. Imagine encouraging tomorrow's scientists and engineers by putting them in touch easily with the women and men who get to step off into space and watch the Earth revolve. When thinking about building business and brand pages, I hope that more companies consider what they can do to help foster education and growth. NASA will definitely implement these kinds of experiences, if their other social media presence is to be a guide, and this speaks well for what else could come about.

The Role of Your Business Page in Doing Business

In watching the early days of people setting up business pages on Google+, I see a lot of people scramble to put together a handful of interesting photographs and then to post several updates about what the company or brand is doing these days. This is to be expected, but it's also just the beginning. To creatively use your business page as part of doing business, following are a few recommendations to consider:

- Think of your business page as a mix of a TV station, a magazine, a telephone, and a business card. As a starting point, frame it like this. You have the opportunity to entertain, to educate, to serve and support, and to convert on your site.

- Consider encouraging more than a few people from varied departments to participate on Google+ and to collaborate on the business page. Sales, marketing, PR, and customer service are easy and obvious choices for people to tap for communicate, but don't stop there. Do your designers want to share some of their inspirations? Could your office manager share a funny story or two about the team? Who else could add flavor to your business pages? And don't forget HR/recruiting.

- Make your customer the hero. Most pages I visit are still focused on themselves. If you make your buyers and users the hero, it's always more compelling. Note how Intel shared "The Sartorialist" as an example of someone using its products. That's a great model.

- Make your About page more about conversion. Make it super easy to point your would-be buyers toward the page on your own site that you feel can best convert them. (And use conversion however you want.) Invite people to subscribe to your email newsletter. Give them simple contact information for follow-up.

- Maintain a Team circle that you will share with the people who circle your business page. Share this circle and update it regularly so that people can circle the individuals in your company that represent the brand, as well. This won't be the right advice for everyone, but leave that to your discretion.

- When posting links to your site or blog, add something to the post on Google+. Don't simply post links. Instead, invite even more interaction by summing up the article or post with some more information. People want more than your rehashed website. They want a unique interaction with you on whichever social platform they use.

- Be the #1 voice in your comments section. Thank people, where appropriate. Respond to questions or requests for help. Realize the multipurpose nature of comments and how some people will ask purchasing questions, whereas others might challenge your policies and methods, whereas others still might be interested in customer service concerns. If you have your marketing team answering all these different needs, the team must be educated about how to help manage the various communications that might arise there.

- Participate on a personal level and not just a business/brand level. Just because you have a business page doesn't mean you have to steer that ship all over Google+ to comment. Use your personal account frequently to comment and respond to posts by those who have circled you on their pages. Be you, a representative of the brand, and not the brand itself. Use that kind of last experience sparingly. People respond much better to other people than they do to a corporate logo.

As I've said at many other points in the book, realize that these bits of advice work differently for different groups and depending on your strategy. Not everything I recommend will be useful to your model, but with a little work, you can modify it for your needs.

A Robust Business Card

As I've said since Google+ launched (and had to say quite often before business pages were implemented), the business page doesn't make you a business person. It's a robust business card. YOU do business by being a human, by representing the brand, and by encouraging interactions of value to both you and your customer or prospect. Camping out on your business page waiting for people to come and interact is like owning a shop and never setting foot onto the sidewalk or visiting any other shops in town.

Social networking tools such as Google+ enable you to be the best digital shop-keeper in the world. You can wander out of your perfect shop (your primary website) and onto the "sidewalk" (social networks), where you can interact with people who might consider your product or service for their own needs. Your goal is to connect with those people where they are, on their pages, on their own sites, and, if conversations go well, to invite them back to interact with your business page, as if you've handed them an interesting, engaging, and interactive business card.

The opportunities to do interesting business here are vast. You should start early, practice often, and see what works. And in one final note, realize that by starting a business page, you should have in place a crisis plan, a few legal possibilities considered, a policy about how to interact with competitors, and many more bits of social business governance. The number one problem with social network business presence is a lack of rough guidelines and plans for what to do with the space and how to respond to the outlier issues that can arise.

Use these pages well, and you can build another great tool to help your company amplify the human digital channel. By building an outpost on Google+, you can potentially increase search rankings, participate with thoughtful users, and use the multitude of tools available to illuminate a new view of your business for your customers and prospects to see.

Feeling Lucky?

It's important to start this chapter by explaining that I'm not an expert in search. I understand the value of search. I know enough about it that I don't make the big mistakes that one can make when constructing a website (no all-Flash sites, for instance). But I also know enough to realize that what Google+ offers you for business above any other opportunity is the chance to improve your search results because Google indexes the publicly shared content you create on Google+.

That means when you post something on Google+ about "How to Pick a Home Improvement Contractor," and the information has lots of great advice that gets shared with people who are interested in this material (and somewhere it has a link back to your site), you can potentially start to see the benefits of that sooner than later. Because Google is actively patrolling Google+ for interesting content that others might want to find via search, you have the chance to get information that's useful to your type of buyer out to the world.

Neither Facebook, Twitter, nor LinkedIn make it easy for Google to do this, by the way. Google no longer indexes Twitter, and it never had access to information inside of Facebook. Because more people use Google to search the web for information than any other search engine, if you do the majority of your online business marketing inside of Facebook, Twitter, and LinkedIn, you miss the potential to reach people who use Google to find you.

This isn't to say that Google+ is all you need to improve your search rankings. If you spend money on a search engine optimization (SEO) already, you won't necessarily be able to cut that budget and just throw a few posts together for Google+. However, spending money simply on SEO without working on organic search value is a waste of money. It is like buying vitamins and protein supplements but then never exercising or eating well. You have to do the hard work to make the supplemental work mean anything.

Home Bases, Outposts, and Search

A fear is that Google+ search results might trump your own website's search rankings. When you Google "chris brogan," you can see my Google+ page come up in the ranks, encroaching on my own site, chrisbrogan.com. In my case, it's not terribly significant because I make it easy for people to contact me. But if your home base is a site that converts people to buy your product, you probably don't want Google+ to creep up in the ranks against you.

One way to keep your primary website the main search result is to be sure not to use the same search terms on your posts on Google+. Another way is to be sure to link back to your primary site and pages far more often than you ever point someone to material you create in Google+. You might also keep mentions of your brand name down on Google+, if you worry that it might take away search relevancy to your primary site. (Again, I'm not a search engine expert or even a decent amateur, but this is a suggestion that comes to mind as possibly helpful. It won't hurt.)

In essence, you work hard to keep the "home base" of your main site as the primary search result for those things you hope to rank for, and use Google+ as your outpost and make posts there a way to guide people to your offerings. More about this in a moment, but first, look at some professionals who can help you better understand how Google+ might impact search.

Social Signals

If you notice that all the big names in SEO are actively trying out Google+ and experimenting, you can see that something important is going on. One of the changes search deals with is how Google weighs the value of links shared via social networks versus links shared via blogs and websites.

Google (the search engine, not Google+ the social network) looks at many factors to decide which web page to promote as the most relevant to someone's search. Some of these traits include understanding how many other sites have linked to a certain page, what text they used when explaining the link, the value of the sites linking to a page, and more.

I asked Danny Sullivan from Search Engine Land to explain how social signals work. This is when Google looks at how people use social networks to point people to a certain page. Danny has been active on Google+ since day 2 and has been working just as hard as all the other top search experts to uncover what matters most. Here's what Danny had to say:

> "Google already looks at social signals as a way to influence its results. Social connections on Google+ are looking like one of the most important of these—and potentially might be more important than gathering links.
>
> Being 'friends' with someone on Google+ means that your search results, if you're logged in, are heavily influenced by what they like and share. Things you wouldn't see in the top results can get pushed higher.
>
> A good example of this was with Ford. It's one of the few companies currently allowed to have a 'brand presence' on Google+. By being friends with Ford, I found that suddenly, they were ranking in the top results for 'cars' in my search results—something that didn't happen when [it was] logged out.
>
> Being friends, in this case, was the number one ranking factor for them doing well, for my results. So being on Google+, having people like you, follow you, is one of the best new SEO techniques out there."

There are many points to consider in what Danny has uncovered. It *does* matter who you add to your circles because Google now uses information it collects about those people to influence what information it gives you when you search. This has implications, obviously.

In Danny's example, being "friends" with Ford Motor Company made generic searches for "cars" rank Ford higher than other brands. That's a huge company with huge competition. You can see this trickling down to smaller companies with even less brand awareness, and suddenly the people you friend, what they search, and how they react to your online presence influences what you buy.

From there, we get into the most important takeaway, as Danny explains it. If being "friends" becomes the #1 ranking factor and is so influential, it suddenly matters that people add you to *their* circles. How do you get added? You provide interesting information, and you respond to their comments and mentions. So, decades later, Dale Carnegie's book on winning friends and influencing people might now turn out to have some monetary implications.

What is the ROI of using a tool like Google+? Well, if what Danny Sullivan explains is any indication, it seems useful to have people add you to their circles, because that impacts the results they see in Google. It's a lot to consider. It means that if you're Dell, you might not just want people to circle Michael Dell, but you want them to circle Richard Binhammer, Lionel Menchaca, and any of the many other Dell employees with individual accounts on Google+. The more people circled from a company who share more and more links to a Dell site or product would then influence that person's search results for computers and so on.

Shifting Sands

Rand Fishkin, CEO and co-founder of SEOMoz, is another search engine expert I admire and frequently read. One of my favorite projects that Rand does is Whiteboard Friday, where he and others shoot videos that talk about SEO and explain it to us novices. I can then talk to other people who *do* know about SEO, tell them these things I see in the videos, and seem like I know enough to get help. It works for me.

When I asked Rand for his thoughts, it was clear that he didn't want to be pinned down in a book about how Google+ impacts search because everything moves so quickly. (I understand this sentiment because this is the first time I've ever written about a software platform in any depth, and I'm naturally nervous about how much will change in the next several months.) But Rand's response is useful because it lets us know that we have to stay alert about how Google experiments with search and the impact that Google+ has.

Here's what Rand says:

> "As of today, Google+ directly influences the rankings of pages and sites in Google in two ways. First, pages shared on the Google+ social network appear to be crawled and indexed by Google's search engine very quickly (within an hour, often faster). Second, pages that are +1'd may appear higher in the rankings to anyone in your Google 'social network,' which can include connections from Google+ itself, as well as Twitter, Facebook, Quora, LinkedIn, and others.
>
> Some important caveats do apply, though. Google has been rapidly experimenting with and changing how +1 and the Google+ network influence

rankings (when, where, how, through whom, and so on). The most direct impact on rankings through +1s in a searcher's 'social network' also seem to be far stronger closer to the time of that +1 and sometimes (though not consistently) fade away thereafter. Google+ and the use of social data in search results are still both in their infancy, and professionals in the search + social marketing spheres anticipate plenty of changes ahead."

Simply by posting a link to a page on Google+, you influence how quickly that page is found by Google (the search engine) and how rapidly someone might find that page through searching the web. Sometimes, speed is of the essence. If you want to take advantage of news, for instance, as a catalyst for selling a product, you might find this is a useful piece of information. But in any case, getting your page indexed and crawled by Google faster is a benefit. It lets people find you sooner instead of later.

Remember also that Google has implemented the +1 button as something to be used all over the web, and not only on Google+. Some of the information Google collects and weighs comes from this, as well, so that's not covered in what you do inside of Google+. This search engine stuff is tricky.

How People Come to Matter

Brian Chappell wrote an interesting article about how Google+ might or might not impact SEO (http://www.ignitesocialmedia.com/seo/google-plus-seo/). The most evident and interesting point is that Google+ is trying to solve the challenge of understanding how people pass trusted information versus how sites and pages pass information. Brian says this about Circles, for instance: "Basically Circles can be seen as a vote for people, like links are a vote for websites. This enables Google to better understand the influencers within its network."

Simply understanding who you've added to your circles (and who have added you to theirs) tells Google more about who you trust and how you value that data. This goes back to what Danny Sullivan was saying, and it gives us a hint about how to get real, tangible value from Google+: The more people validate us by adding us to their circles, the more it shows Google that people value the quality of what we post and share.

Does this mean you should rush out and seek to be part of yet another numbers game? It depends on what you want from your experience on Google+. Remember, you can't make people add you to a circle, so your only real option is to be interesting. (You could beg, but that wouldn't be attractive, would it?)

On the other side, perhaps you should consider who you've added to your circles because if this is how Google starts to understand who you value, it might be interesting to know how that impacts your search efforts and any other measures of influence that Google might try to understand.

Circle who you want, and don't worry about how this impacts any search algorithms. To be circled by influential people, say interesting and unique things. Be helpful. Comment on their posts with meaningful information. Or just leave it to chance and focus on creating useful material for your core audience. (That's what many people do.)

Serving Suggestions for Using Google+ to Improve Your Search Results

Building search value inside Google+ simply requires that you create posts with terms that others might tend to search for later in Google. Not unlike other web pages, there's no value to stuffing the post with repetitive search terms (Google actually discounts for actions like this), but if you write something that would appeal to a human reader, chances are you'll have created something within the parameters of what Google considers okay. Do this with an example.

If you sell lobsters, for instance, you might write a post that looks like this:

Maine Lobster Shipped Anywhere

When the team at JR Booker's Lobster says it ships lobsters anywhere, it really means it. It recently received an order for a half-dozen lobsters to be sent up to the International Space Station! The little fellers are going to be astronauts!

Here's a picture of the lobsters before putting them in the special packing container that can ensure their fresh arrival into space.

(with an appropriate picture, of course)

This is (obviously?) a fictitious example. I'm not sure anyone's had lobsters in space. But in this case, the post is titled with something that might be searched on in Google, "Maine Lobster" but also "Lobster Shipped." "It ships lobsters anywhere" is in the first line of the post, in case that's what someone might ask about. Other things could be added, such as the company's phone number, a street address, and an email address. But then it would start to look like an ad. That works sometimes but is not so great all the time.

But overall, this post might be of interest to the stream at large. It has some search terms embedded in it, near the name of the company, and hopefully with some potential for being found useful to someone who stumbles upon the post out in the larger world of Google search. The goal to make this useful to a potential buyer should be met. But you can consider a few other areas.

Ensure that some of the links in your profile use good anchor text. (The blue words of the links should be words that relate to a search term that you hope someone will find valuable.) For instance, I sell a product called "Blog Topics," so I put a link to that offering with the anchor text "writing advice and blog topics." Try this. It won't hurt.

Use Your Profile

Although covered in a previous chapter, make sure your profile on Google+ has several ways for people to contact you. To continue with the previous example, if you're James Richmond Booker, and you run JR Booker's Lobsters, you'll want the company website listed in the links on the right of your profile. You'll want your introduction to talk about how your company ships lobsters anywhere. You'll want to enable the "send email" function, if you are willing to check your email often. You'll probably want to put your phone number in the profile area and list address information to your store or stores.

In this case, the profile can become the static ad for your company on one level. But don't forget to leave in the personal information to draw people to want to get to know you when they're not in the market for a lobster. Talk about your family, your hobbies, or where you live and what you're into besides fishing for lobsters. Make your profile personable but also useful to your business at the same time.

Taking Full Advantage of Google+ to Help Your Business

When it comes to search, realize that Google+ enables you to post photos, video, text, links, and location data. All these post types enable a prospective buyer to learn more about you, and when you post this information to your public stream, you're giving Google permission to index and crawl that information and thus help others find it outside of Google+. You can post location data to your restaurants, one post after the other, until it's clear where you're located. Throw in a picture or a text post of the week's specials, and you have something that might be useful to people.

The caution is that you don't want to look like a steady stream of advertisements, especially not on your primary personal account. It's asking to be uncircled. However, if you can take that kind of interesting information that's useful for search and turn it into stories that draw people's attention, you have something. Like the lobster company example, the idea is to make news and stories out of your business. Also, don't forget about the effectiveness of video testimonials about your business with clients. This doesn't have to be award-winning material. Just shoot less than two minutes of you asking a customer a few questions using a camcorder and post it to YouTube. Post it to Google+ with some information, being clear to add in information that is search-worthy, and you have another opportunity to help people inside and outside of Google+ to find your business and start a relationship.

Always think about ways you can make a story out of business. Do you have the most amazing banjo-playing woman in the packing department? Then shoot a video of her great work and post it up, explaining how cool the people who deliver your products are. Do you have a CEO who runs off to play rugby with the Irish Fireman's League? (The CEO of the company I used to work for does this, and I thought he was crazy!) Post photos from his recent match, and point out that your CEO can kick other companies' CEOs' butts. (Why not?)

Make stories out of your customers. If someone uses your product and gets great results, make him the hero. Ask for a photo. Ask for a quick video. (A photo is probably a bit more likely.) Write the story with more information geared toward the customer and less about you. Don't make the story look like this: "Were it not for her smart decision to use the Greppo 3100, Janie Stamper would be homeless!" Instead, make it like this: "Janie Stamper is the best apple carver in all of Ohio, maybe the WORLD! She can get amazing results out of her Greppo 3100 and is the envy of church bazaars everywhere!" The difference, quite subtly, is that the story is about how amazing Janie is, and not how your tool is what makes her carve apples better than the other apple carvers. You with me?

Stay Organic

Above all else, don't worry about mechanical means to try to boost your search results on Google+. Don't look into paying people who offer to improve your ranking or who offer to get you more followers. Remember: It's not how many people who circle you that matters, nearly as much as it's about the quality of the person who circles you. Besides, there are many ways to get in trouble with search ranking when you consider using inorganic means to get there. Why risk doing something that causes Google to remove any result relevancy to your sites or posts?

Tell great stories. Write interesting posts that get influential people to consider circling you, and work on your own quality of information more than anything else. That's what can get you the most benefit from using Google+.

If you're interested in learning more about search, check out Danny Sullivan's and Rand Fishkin's blogs:

- http://searchengineland.com

- http://seomoz.org

You can find other great sources out there, but these are two of the guys to pay attention to when you aren't sure what to do and when you want to improve search results. Search matters.

16

Tactics

When I've worn you down a bit, you'll finally say, "Okay, you've worn me down. What now?" My answer invariably starts with the question, "What's the goal?" Here are some potential goals you can use Google+ to achieve:

- Improved searchability and discovery of your main website

- Lead generation

- Informational offerings to enhance the buying process

- Lead nurturing

- Prospecting

- Customer service and community management

- Direct selling

- Traffic enhancement to your main site

That's a decent swath of business goals. What would you do? This chapter shares some "recipes" that you can adapt to your own needs. These can be in-the-weeds tactical stuff, so if you have a larger company, you might need to add some steps to make them work according to your processes. If you have a smaller company, you should do fine. Let's walk through some of these.

Searchability

If searchability is your goal, then the game is content creation. What's going to help? Well, let's start with what's not going to help. If you post frequent spam or junk content to your Google+ page (note that I don't necessarily mean your business page— you can apply this logic to your personal page or your business page), you'll probably get uncircled.

There are two goals when using Google+ for better searchability: to get people to find your information useful so that they circle you and to provide content that helps people find your site and your primary business. To accomplish these goals, you need to create interesting, useful content that also helps people who are searching for what you sell to find you. For example, if you're selling homes in Portland, Maine, then you might take a page from the Corcoran Group's rulebook, and write daily posts about interesting things to see and do in Portland, such as a trip to the Old Port to have brunch at the Portland Harbor Hotel. Take a few pictures and talk about the neighborhood and the kinds of people who are there. Let people see themselves in the setting.

Do you think it takes a long time to write pieces like this? This isn't the case at all. You snap a few pictures. You think about what someone who might move to the area would want to know about and you write about it like you're that person's tour guide (which you are). You also might mention "great places to live in Portland." That phrase or term becomes something that gets sucked into Google.com's search engine. Soon, your post about how fun it is to get lobster omelets at the Portland Harbor Hotel is highly ranked as a searched article. Who wrote it? Why, the best real estate company in Portland, of course.

Do you see how this plays out for you if you are a realtor? Don't show your listings. Don't end with a hard sell. Don't push that you're an award-winning real estate professional. Just let people see that you're telling a story. This will find you prospects and it will improve your searchability. Modify this to whatever you sell. If you sell mountain bikes, write about the places where people use these. Want some ideas about this kind of thing? Look up Chris Zoller from PolarUSA on Google+. His examples are great.

Lead Generation

If you want to get more sales, there are certainly ways to do so via your Google+ page or even via your comments on other people's posts. If someone has to make a decision about smartphones and how to pick a good one, maybe you're Esteban Contreras at Samsung USA. You might comment that you're obviously biased as a representative of Samsung, but you are there to answer any questions about your products and you're even willing to point people to third-party reviews or comparisons. Yes, this is "bespoke" selling, one person at a time, but it's also the kind of story that gets around. It doesn't take long for people to realize that you're there with a passion for your product or service, but you're not going to try and be "that guy."

Notice that the first example I give you is about lead generation comments on someone else's page. Remember that selling and doing business on Google+ isn't just about creating content. It's most definitely useful for you to pay attention to what people say. That big search box at the top of the website enables you to cook up searches for your product name, your competitors' names, or a phrase or situation that might signal to someone a need for what you sell. Spending some time searching the posts of others is a great way to generate leads.

Here are a few other ways to generate leads:

- Host live Hangouts where you do product demonstrations. Imagine getting a celebrity guest to demonstrate your product every 20 minutes for 4 hours. Can you turn Google+ into QVC for the day? I bet you can.

- Post giveaways and contests.

- Write articles that identify a need that your product solves.

- Post photos of happy customers.

- Post YouTube videos of interviews with happy customers.

- Post behind-the-scene videos of how you do what you do. (Dogfish Head beer has some great behind-the-scene videos.)

- Host live meet ups, where you use the Location feature to invite the first five people to find you at a location to get a free whatever.

In all these cases, when it comes to creating information, the goal is to move people from a good experience on your post or your Hangout to a more recognizable sales funnel for your organization. If it's an email address or a phone number, then invite people back to your main site or to wherever you intend to capture this information. Don't leave the experience solely on Google+.

You'll note that I have two different ways of tackling business back to back here. In the previous searchability example, I said that one might not want to push for a conversion to the main website at the end of the post, but in lead generation, I'm all for it. To me, there's a balance. People won't rush to your lead-generation posts, except to satisfy the nature of the experience you're offering. With a searchability-minded post, what I want people to do is think of you as an informational resource. That's the distinction. While we're on "information," let's look at that in more detail.

Informational Offerings

I've been getting into making music lately. As part of this process, I'm buying some software and hardware to help me create it. This has led me to do a lot of research online. I've found two things. First, I've found that companies making YouTube videos of their products and services are few and far between, but those that do capture a lot more of my attention and thus, they capture my intention to buy. The second thing I've found is that most of the content created by companies is created by marketing departments and is unusable by the people who might be on the cusp of making a purchase. In other words, turn my griping into your blueprint for business success.

Though it's not heavily on Google+, if you look at Native Instruments on YouTube, you can see some examples of great video of informational offerings. On YouTube, look up "Moldover with Traktor F1" and you'll see what I mean. It's a demonstration by someone using the company's product, and it gives you a sense of what you can accomplish with it. Bring this mindset back to what you can post on YouTube, and then what you can put into Google+, and you'll have a winner.

Depending on what you sell, there's always something that people want or need to know that can make their experience with your product or service better. If you sell running shoes, maybe you can post videos about how to know when it's time to get a new pair (which happens faster than most runners believe). If you offer lawn and garden services, maybe you can create a post, video, or series of pictures that explains how homeowners can stretch the time between visits from your company (which obviously gets you fewer sales, but also shows off that you're a professional and that you're not going to sell people something they don't need).

The main goal here is to inform people in a space that's larger than just your product. Even though the Native Instrument examples that I cited at the beginning are specific to that tool, people who might use that tool (such as me) might think, "Wow, I can do something like that with this tool?" This leads me further into the purchasing funnel. Note, the competitors to Native Instruments don't make many videos or informational products, and I can tell you as a potential buyer that this impacts my decision to buy. How does that relate to you and your competitors?

Realize that the goal is to make brief informational videos and textual posts more frequently. People don't have all day. The beauty in making this information visible on Google+ is that people who are your potential buyers are likely to +1 this data (signaling to Google that you created something of value), or they might even share your post with their own following, especially if you've addressed the larger ecosystem and not just your own particular product. This means that not just one potential buyer will find your information. When that buyer chooses to share it with others, who might then become a potential buyer? It's magic.

Lead Nurturing

Whenever I corner a salesperson, I ask him this question, "What are you doing to nurture leads before the sale?" Most say, "Uh, I call them up and ask them if they have any questions I can help them with," or in other cases, "I invite them to shows they might like or to dinner." Very little has happened to make lead nurturing get better. And yet, with a service such as Google+, if you've got leads that you'd like to keep warm and help guide to the finish line of a purchase, these tools work great.

If your potential lead is already on Google+, you can "read over his shoulder" and learn about his moods or thoughts by looking at what he posts on Google+. If you're about to make a sales call and you read that your lead just had to leave work to book an emergency trip across the country to deal with a sick relative, you'll know that today's not the day to have that call. If you note that your lead is snapping a lot of photos from Memphis and that's also the home base of your competitor, you might step up your game. It's like mind reading, if the potential customer is already there.

But what if the potential customer is not already there? Another way to nurture leads is to invite your potential customers to use Google+ as a way to learn more. Invite them into discussion forums about the space you serve. Invite them to talk with the people who make your product or service. Invite them to become part of your information-sharing initiative where you share the offerings we created previously. Giving people a reason to show up to your page on Google+ is a great way to keep people interested and warm on the way to the purchase phase, and it's a great way to be available to answer any questions or remove any obstacles to purchase.

Prospecting

If you want one of my biggest secrets, it's that you can do amazing prospecting on Google+. The best potential client for my own company is a mid- to larger-sized business that seeks to improve its business efforts on the digital channel. I spend 40 to 60 percent of my time on Google+ inside of search prospecting for potential clients that fit that description. Sometimes, I find someone who works for the company I'm trying to work with. Other times, I find someone who is voicing a need that I know I can satisfy with my offerings. In all cases, the ability to prospect is one of the best reasons to use the service. People spend a part of everyday indicating their needs to you via social networking channels such as Google+. It's up to you to identify how you can serve those needs, and then help them achieve their goals.

The ability to "cook a search" on Google+ is useful. You can go to the search bar, give it a bunch of parameters, and then you save that search for future uses. Thus, whenever you have few moments to "check the traps," you can go and see whether someone has communicated a need that matches your ability to serve. For instance, if you sell travel packages or you rent luxury properties, you can search on variants of the question, "Where should I go for vacation?" Believe me, there are many people out there putting that question to the test.

But what if you have no idea which search terms to use? Start with the third-party service FindPeopleOnPlus.com. This site collects publicly-declared demographics from millions of users on Google+, which then gives you the chance to search for people by location, age, occupation, gender, and several other pieces of data. It's one of the single best third-party sites for Google+ at present. If Google+ made this data available to me for sale, I would buy it in a heartbeat, but in the meantime, FindPeopleOnPlus.com is doing a great job of scraping data and compiling it so we can find where our potential buyers might be.

Customer Service and Community Management

In this specific case, I find that many companies use Facebook for their online community management outpost. This is probably the strongest suit for a business to use for Facebook. But I feel that Google+ is working in this direction and that you'll see a porting of some of these communities over to Google+, depending on how adoption continues to track. Companies such as Dell are already actively trying Google+ as another outpost for managing communities, probably because Michael Dell himself is using the platform. You'll also see the cable company Comcast on Google+ working to replicate a much-covered digital brand of customer service.

I haven't seen many companies rushing in to do this yet. As business pages are still fairly nascent in their functionality and as users are still dipping their toes into the waters of Google+ to understand what they want to do with the service, people are not exactly rushing to have this experience on Google+ yet. But that "yet" is just a "matter of time;" there is opportunity for you.

My advice here is to build a community that encompasses your product or service but that doesn't exclude competitors. I know this is antithetical to most business practices today, but it also has the biggest potential for a win. If you're talking to beer drinkers, for example, there are maybe two types of beer drinkers: those who like beer in general and brand purists. Brand purists aren't all that useful to a community platform because they're simply going to argue endlessly about how their brand is the best. But that first category—people who like beer (I fall into this demographic)—are the people who love both Dogfish Head and Molson/Coors products. They just like trying out interesting and delicious beer.

So, are those generalists like me more willing to join a Molson Golden brand page, are we more likely to join a Dogfish Head page, or would we rather join a "Beer Lovers Unite" page? Hint: The conversation on the "Beer Lovers Unite" page would likely be the most interesting. I'm sure we'll talk about making beer, about the process, about all kinds of interesting beers we've yet to try. We'll learn why Baxter Brewing sells only cans and why Molson/Coors helps out fledgling craft brewers who might eventually create beers that compete with their own. Doesn't that sound much more fun than talking about a single brand?

If you're the owner of such a brand, however, this is a twitchy thing. If you work in Detroit in the U.S., for example, and you work for GM, it's probably not great to drive a Honda CR-V. At least, that's what the prevailing sentiment has been. This way of thinking, however, has run its course. There's a huge opportunity to capture even more business by supporting the space at large. If you're Molson/Coors and you beat everyone else to creating the "Beer Lovers Unite" page, you're going to come off as a genius compared to the lesser-trafficked, single-brand sites.

Direct Selling

If you sell tutoring of any kind, Google+ is a great platform for you. Assume you sell nutritional coaching. You can have private one-on-one video conferences with your clients no matter where they are via Google Hangouts. If people are willing to participate in small groups, you can even see up to nine clients at a time. Selling this kind of service is getting more common on the platform. I've seen guitar instructors, yoga teachers, life coaches, and even a few chefs sell their services live and via Google+. Because Google+ doesn't have a specific payment mechanism, you have to do these transactions outside of the system on Google Money, Amazon Payments, or PayPal. But that's not too difficult to manage. If you don't send people an invite to your Hangout, they can't join, so you don't have to worry about keeping people out. To me, this is a great opportunity, especially as you can do all the prospecting and lead generation on the site, wait for people to comment, and then offer them an immediate sale or gratification (if you're there when they comment live) that turns into direct business. I've seen some people do this and it's exciting. There's just so much more opportunity.

Affiliate marketing does over $13 billion dollars in business and it's growing. This is when someone has an audience, doesn't have a product of their own, but markets or sells a product on a company's behalf to that audience. For instance, I don't make luggage, but I have sold the Eagle Creek carry-on bags via my websites for years because I think it's a great product. My effort makes me a few extra hundred bucks a month, which isn't a lot, but it amounts to never flinching when I feel like buying a lobster dinner for friends. You can create posts that explain the product or service that you're selling, and you can entice people to consider clicking your links for potential purchase.

Do note that it's important to disclose the links you've created are affiliate links, especially if you're in the U.S., where the FTC has some strict rules about disclosure of such relationships. That said, it's as simple as putting the phrase "affiliate link" directly after the links you use to point people to your product. If it's a picture or a link at the bottom of the post, just include the phrase "affiliate link" somewhere in the body of the post that precedes the link.

Traffic Enhancement to Your Main Site

Traffic enhancement is probably the most common use of Google+ for businesses right now, especially if you've built a media element to what you do and if you're a publication or media property of some kind. This is essentially when you post a link to your website from Google+ to highlight an article or post you've written. At the time of writing this book, there aren't any automated tools that schedule and post this kind of information; however, you can easily write posts, point a link to your website, and then click publish.

The best practice I've seen, however, is to write a little something or create a useful précis that leads people to consider clicking your link. Ask a question and point out that your thoughts about the answer are on the other side of the link. Do something to generate interest before people click through.

A primary concern, oddly, is that people might comment on the Google+ posting and not on the blog. Yes, technically, this is like splitting potential social proof, as you'd love to show that your most recent post has 50 comments or more; however, if you get 10 comments on Google+ and 40 on the post itself, count yourself lucky and be sure to reply to people where they posted their ideas. If they post thoughts about your article on the Google+ post that shared it, reply to them on Google+. This also encourages more comments and interaction from others.

There's More

Obviously, I picked only a small subset of the ways people can use Google+ to do business. My intention was to create several tactical approaches to consider when using these tools to build your own business. As stated at the beginning of this chapter, you might have to tweak some of these ideas if you're working for a larger company. For smaller companies, your goal is to ensure that people feel like they have what they need to make a decision. It's that simple.

17

Recipes for Using Google+

Throughout time, when people are faced with something new, the way they learn to integrate those new things into their lives is through recipes. During World War II, house-wives (hey, that's what it was at the time) were offered all kinds of substandard cuts of meat at the grocers because the Allies needed the "good stuff" overseas with them. Thus, women were asked to prepare liver, beef tongue, and tripe. When faced with a giant purple tongue of a cow, there wasn't an immediate and obvious response, and most didn't have information about what to do with these unusual cuts of meat.

Enter recipe cards. Magazines and newspapers went into overdrive creating ideas on how to turn that beef tongue into something the kids would eat. (I'm going to go out on a very thick and heavy limb and say that I doubt any kids really were down with the tongue, recipes be damned.) Truly, this is how massive national behavior was changed in the U.S. and U.K. (and elsewhere): recipes.

In the first edition of the book, I provided serving suggestions for how one might use Google+. Though I don't want to focus on the step-by-step of using the technology, I felt that you might benefit from having some recipes for using the service and adding more value to your business. I'm not going to profess that my recipes are as world-changing as the World War II recipes were. Instead, I'll say that if you've been sitting around feeling as if, "I'm here, now what?" then I can help alleviate the anxiety that comes with that feeling. You've got business interests and I can help you think of Google+ in a different light that might be of use to you and your business.

These recipes aren't in any particular order. There isn't a recipe one and a recipe two. Instead, I've just poked around and looked at what might be useful. Some of these won't apply to you. Others will require tweaking to make it work for you. Just like a recipe book for food, you'll have to "salt to taste." That said, these recipes are ways to squeeze more out of Google+.

How to Find More People to Circle on Google+

The first complaint of most people who join Google+ is "None of my friends are here." This is the equivalent of buying a refrigerator and saying, "There's no food in here." You have to look around to find people of value to circle, and though they may not be your "friends" from other social networks, why would your immediate thought be to replicate what you've already built elsewhere? Instead, focus on finding people with like interests. Here are ways to do that:

- Visit Find People on Plus (http://findpeopleonplus.com). You can sort potential people and businesses by location (if you're a local business, this is helpful), by occupation (if you sell to farmers, there are 1,936 people listed with an occupation of farmer), by employer (there are 13,836 people from Wal-Mart on here and 29,248 from IBM), and even by a keyword you dream up. I typed "Batman" and found that 4,291 people have the word "Batman" in their profiles. Realize that Find People on Plus is a third-party application that is scraping Google+ public records to make this site work, so it's not exactly accurate or sanctioned. That said, it works well.

- Use Google+ Search (the little nifty search bar at the top) and plug in whatever term you're hoping to find. You can put in your company name, your competitor, your prospects, or whatever else is interesting to you. I have searched for people involved in the comic books industry, as I've had a lifelong appreciation for comics. Then, I searched for people in the conference venue business, as I put on events. It's fun to spend your time in Search, because you'll find more business there than you will as a result of writing interesting posts on your page. Yes, if you've ever wanted to find a secret that means a lot from a business book, this one secret is the biggest part of social media's misunderstanding: it's not what you're posting, it's what you're discovering and acting upon that will make you money.

 Tip

You can save searches that you've typed into the Search bar, and those will show up on Explore.

- Try friendsurfing. If you want to find interesting people, start with the people you've already deemed interesting. Kevin Kelly (https://plus.google.com/+kevinkelly) helped launch *Wired Magazine* and the legendary WELL online community, and among other things, he is trying to categorize every species on Earth (because who wouldn't?). A quick glance of who he has in his circles pulls up quite a few mutual friends who are equally as interesting: Jeff Jarvis the media scholar, Craig Newmark of Craigslist fame, Tim O'Reilly of O'Reilly media, and Nick Bilton of the *New York Times* for starters. Thus, if you find Kevin interesting, you'll probably like his friends. Voilà, you have found more interesting people to circle.

- Visit the Explore page. Maybe you're not sure who to circle. Maybe you just want to browse around to start. Go to Explore (https://plus.google.com/explore) and see what comes up. There's an area for what's trending on Google+, what is currently "hot," people or pages you might find interesting, and more. This is very much Potpourri.

How to Be Ready for Business on Google+

It's astounding how many hundreds of profiles I've reviewed in the writing of this book (maybe a thousand or more, but I'm trying not to sound obsessive), who have not filled out their profile in a way that is conducive to helping them do business. Several have left no way to contact them. Some have left it up to the Google+ Contact button only (which at the time of this writing is a tiny icon in the upper right corner of one's profile near a much more colorful button, and could be mistaken for many things that aren't a message bar). Here is a recipe for how to fill out your profile:

A lot of people seem to fill out their profile as if only grudgingly. Others use the same biography they've splattered all over the web without any sense of the real opportunity. Make your About page work better for you and be ready for the potential of business.

To get started, simply go to your About page, click the Profile button, click the tab for About, and then click Edit Profile. (I made this a standalone step because it's amazing how few people edit their profile after the first day, and several have said it's because they didn't realize how to do it.)

If you haven't put a recent and decent picture of you (not your logo) as your profile picture, fix this. Humans are trained to look at faces. It's one of the only built-in reflexes we have besides breathing upon birth. Just because I'm asked this question a lot, I'll take this moment to say that I don't believe you have to stick with the same avatar all the time, and I'll say that you don't have to use the same picture across all social networks. Yes, it aids with recognition, but it's not a must. If you insist on representing your brand via a logo, then consider using a photo editor to put a small version of your logo in the lower third portion of your avatar, a la Scott Monty of the Ford Motor Company, one of the most tasteful avatars on the web.

For your cover photo, I'd recommend using this splash area for something that is interesting enough to draw attention. I've seen a lot of people stuff their website banner into this area. Here's a secret: Social networks like Google+ are like the liner notes of your primary work. Were you around when music came in LP format on vinyl? One of the lost arts of that world besides art that was more than 12 inches across the square were the liner notes, the parts inside that would afford a chance for the artists to talk about what went into making their work. If you view your opportunity on social networks as a chance to create the liner notes of your real work, it means you're giving people a chance to see the person behind the business. We buy from people we like. If you're a shameless fan of pugs, then be like Jenny Cisney from Kodak and post photos of your dogs at every turn.

If you're like Richard Binnhammer from Dell, you will post photos of you with other people you've spent time with. This is social proof and it means that people coming to the page say, "Wow! There's Richard with this or that person I've read about online somewhere." It's another good way to show people that you have some value in this universe, and it's a visual one, so it's a way of "short-handing" the mental process of ascribing value.

This goes beyond pretty pictures. Your tagline is another part of what helps people understand how you might do business with them. People misunderstand the tagline and think it's a great place to put a witty saying. Sure, you can do that. Or, you can make that line the most compelling possible sentence that will draw people's attention, helping them determine whether or not to do business with you. This is a book on business, so you know what I propose.

At the time of writing this second edition of the book, my tagline has changed because my business has changed. I'm focusing on professionals now more than I'm focusing on entire companies. I still work with people at big companies, but more often, I talk to people with companies of one, two, or ten employees. What do I sell both? The same thing:

> "Working with professionals to do the work they want, craft a clear vision, a plan of action, and build a network of support."

This might not be the best, but it gives you a decent sense of what I'm selling and to whom. There are even some secret code words in there. You might be a marketing manager at Best Buy, but you might *want* to work for the Cirque du Soleil. That's why I help people do the "work they want."

But realize that this is my tagline. It's the first thing one sees on my big About page, but there's something else to address that people see before this in most cases.

On your About page, find the Employment area, and on the current job, put down the company name if it's relevant and what you do for clients and customers. My role currently shows up as this: "HBW: I publish courses and other media to help you grow." It gives you a sense of how I will interact with you as a prospective buyer. Whatever you put on this line is what people will see when they hover over your name. Sometimes, this is the only chance you'll get to make an impression with people. Thus, make sure your first impression is succinct and helpful.

The #1 mistake people make when it comes to filling out this section is listing their employment as "self," because they are self-employed. That says nothing except that you don't have a boss. What do you do for people? That's the information people need.

Your introduction is somewhat obvious. Tell people about what you can do for them. In mine, I expand on a few ways one can do business with me, and then I add a link to my own contact form. In my case, I use a simple form for people to use to reach me. What makes this a power move, however, is that this makes it double-super-extra-better-easy for people to reach you outside of what's built into Google+. If you don't have a contact form on your primary website, you can put an email address here, or you can put another step in place. I've seen some people list a contact telephone number.

Where people get this contact form part wrong is when they make people go from a personal feeling About page to a cold starting point in the corporate funnel. If you want to capture and maintain the human side of business with this move, make sure people can reach you, or when they go to that contact form, include a "I found you via Google+" option or something. The goal is keeping the contact warm and friendly.

The other parts of the About page are also important, but they're a bit more obvious to figure out, except maybe for the links at the bottom. As stated before, keep the profile links as thin as possible. Most people have an inclination to list everywhere on the web they can be found. This becomes a problem that marketers know as the paradox of choice: Give me more than two choices and I'll do nothing. Instead, put one or two links to important sites or locations, and leave it at that. This is how people find you best.

And now, if we've done all this, we're ready for business.

Promoting Yourself and Your Business on Google+

I had an interesting exchange with someone the other day. He complained about a post I wrote, stating that it wasn't all that interesting to him. There's humor in this. He spent how many minutes of his time deciding to critique my post? But then, as any good offended person does instead of shrugging off a critic that shouldn't matter, I went to look at what he posted, given that he's the expert.

Every post, one after the other, was promoting his private networking group. Sometimes, he'd vary it up by promoting a member of the network. None of them had comments. None of them had been shared. None had even been plussed (arg, I hate that verb). Do I think that's useful for his business? Not at all. Is he going to grow a following by beating people with his company's goals every post? Definitely not.

Here's some thoughts for a recipe (some of this echoes what I wrote in other chapters, but some of this is new to this second edition).

- Post no more than four times a day, no fewer than once a day. To keep people attentive to your participation on Google+, you need to stay at least a little bit active in the stream.

- Of those posts, try to vary whether you're writing something self-promotional (or promoting your company's goals) versus something of interest to the type of community you hope to attract. If you were to do four posts a day, I'd recommend 1:4 (one self-promotional piece for every four total posts).

- In your posts, appeal to what might appeal about the space and the people you have the pleasure to serve. The Corcoran Group, for instance, writes about the varied communities and sights of New York City. I don't know that I've ever seen them list a property on Google+, but I know that they are an oft-cited example of someone drawing people's attention in, which gives them the top-of-mind opportunity, should one need a quality property in New York. If you're Joe Sorge of

AJ Bombers fame, you're writing posts of interest to people local to Milwaukee and Madison, Wisconsin, and so there's always a local, community feel to posts. This is the gold standard. You can sell later, you can sell elsewhere, or you can sell sporadically. That's how this particular medium works.

- If you're linking to your new blog post, try asking a good question that encourages a reader to click in and read the post. It turns out "new blog post" isn't exactly an appealing piece of meat to dangle in front of us. Instead, if you asked, "Does your company make this mistake, and how much is it costing you?" Well, now you have my attention, because I'm pretty sure I make that mistake and I want to know how much money I'm losing every second I don't read your post. See?

- The real truth is that it's rarely about how much you post and what you post, but instead, how you interact. You need *something* on your page for people to see and interact with, and you need enough posts to show that the lights are on and that you're participating on Google+. But it's when you "go visiting" and spend time in search and comment elsewhere that you'll find potential business.

On the day I wrote these words, I went searching for people who were looking for conference venue recommendations. It stood to reason that the same people who seek out such things might also need keynote speakers (hey, that's me!), and so I struck up some conversations with people about their businesses, their challenges, and so on. In one case, the person wasn't exactly a fit, so I just did what I could, made an introduction or two, and moved on.

The other is a perfect prospect for what I'm doing, and so I offered to send her a copy of my upcoming book, told her about what I'm capable of doing for conferences like the one she is organizing, and I let her know that I'd be willing to give her my 2012 rates for her 2013 event, if she wanted to proceed. In other words, I did business based on what I saw in search.

I mentioned in a previous recipe (and often when I'm on stage) that most of the exciting business I've booked for myself and clients has come from search and not from what I post. Yes, it's great when someone reads a blog post of mine and realizes that I'm the perfect person for a job. But that happens far less frequently than when I find someone expressing a need that I can solve.

Thus, a backwards secret of promoting yourself might be what you accomplish when commenting and interacting with people about their posts and far less about what you do on your own. You're welcome to disagree with me, but I've seen many examples of this in action. I hope you are one of them.

Hangouts on Google+: The Best Opportunity You Rarely Take

Perhaps the best function of Google+ is the live video hangout. Since the first edition of this book, Google+ has opened up the functionality called Hangouts on Air, which lets you can have up to 10 people as panelists and an unlimited number of viewers. This service works well, has features and functions (that I won't talk a *lot* about), and might be the key to making more business happen. Here's a quick list of what you can use Hangouts to accomplish:

- **Private coaching groups**—Because you control who is invited, you can invite just paying members of your community to a special live experience.

- **Education**—If you're a math tutor, a music teacher, or a yogini, for example, you've got a built-in way to work with remote clients.

- **Exclusive access**—I had the pleasure of interviewing Sir Richard Branson for a magazine cover article and we talked over Skype. Can you imagine how much more powerful the experience might have been had I invited the subscribers of the magazine to a special live Q&A with Branson? It would be magical.

- **Internal meetings**—You can use Google+ for quick team meetings, especially if your company is geographically distributed. You can invite internal members as well as external, because you control who is invited.

- **Tech support via the screen share opportunity**.

- **Musical events**—There are plenty of musicians taking advantage of Google+, and as the company learns about how to create a better experience for these performances, the added features available to musicians (which as of this writing are still in a bit of a trial mode) are definitely something of value. As a business, even if you're not in the music business, you might have an opportunity to promote events like this as a bonus to your customers.

The possibilities are endless. You're your own television station, should that be of interest. I've done almost every variant and have found it useful to my business. Do you want to start? Here's a recipe card to get more out of the experience:

- The equipment required to do a live video hangout is simply an Internet connection and a webcam. This is sometimes tricky for people, but as technology improves and as almost every laptop now comes with a decent enough camera in the lid, we're getting closer to this being ubiquitous.

- It is useful to point out that if you want better video quality, plugging your computer directly into the Internet connection is a lot better than Wi-Fi for such productions. It's a lot less likely that you'll be successful as a host of such an experience if you stream from Starbucks, where you'll share Wi-Fi with another 20 people, versus from your own office or home. In the case of people working in larger companies, sometimes, your network team has methods to separate out dedicated Internet connectivity for your needs. Check with them. Oh, and by not checking with people ahead of time, if you are hogging the bandwidth, this is a great way to have the plug pulled by an automated network monitoring tool without you or anyone else being notified. (It has to happen only once for you to put this on your recipe card.)

- I mentioned that all you need is a laptop and an Internet connection. If you were going to move up to the next level in creating a decent video hangout, start with sound. The weird secret to good video is that great audio helps give the sense that a video is of quality. I use the Blue Yeti microphone (http://scrt.co/blueyeti), which plugs into your laptop's USB and works in a few different modes. It costs around $100, which is worth it, if you want great sound.

- Next comes lighting. If you want a great hangout, make sure that you're lit well. This means that the source of light on you is on your face and not behind you (what I call witness protection lighting). I don't cover this in depth here, but if you Google (the search not the plus pages) "three pointing lighting," and watch a quick YouTube video, you'll see what I'm talking about. Even if you do something like this, you'll be ahead.

- After this, it's important to consider access when you start a hangout. If you invite the public, the public might show up. It's useful. Instead, if you've done well with choosing circles, you can invite specifically who you want to bring to your event.

Marketers tend to make a mistake on this part of the recipe. As we are trained to want to grab everyone we can, we mistake the public for this. This is rarely useful. Why? Because the public includes "bored people who want to raise hell and cause a problem." Your hangout will suffer accordingly.

Instead, just select useful and pertinent people to invite, or at the most, invite "Extended circles," which are the people you've chosen to follow plus the people they've chosen to follow.

- Aim for brevity. An hour-long event is quite a tax on attendees' attention. If you can do what you're seeking to accomplish in 20 minutes, that would be ideal. If you must, 30 minutes is be a good upper limit. The reason is that most people will view this from their laptop or desktop, in an environment that doesn't really afford people a lot of time. As much as you want to think that everyone's eagerly awaiting your one hour of great information about X, they are probably more than likely only up for 20 minutes of live viewing.

  If you want to break that time barrier, one way to do this is to do *some* of the event live and offer the rest to watch on YouTube or via a download or something. This gives people a best of both worlds opportunity.

- Another useful way to use Google Hangouts is to use the collaborative tools such as shared documents or a shared white board. Shared documents can be used to collaborate over a report or document in which you want to see in real time the other person's edits or changes. You can use white board to talk through a design element with someone or to discuss a flow of events.

How to Use Google+ for Sales

This recipe is difficult to create because sales can cover a lot of ground. If you're trying to push your latest $9 ebook, it's a lot easier than if you're working on selling a $300,000 ride share on a private jet. And yet, there are opportunities for you to use Google+ to sell on either side of that spectrum. Here is the recipe for how to do this regardless of the spectrum:

- Remember that research is one of the greatest ways you can use Google+. Let's say you need to sell to Michael Dell, the CEO of Dell. By following him on Google+, you can find out what he's interested in on a given day and you can find out what kind of mood he might be in, if only by reading between the lines. That's one way to do it.

  You should also pay attention to other signs. If someone is using the check-in options and you see that they're visiting Memphis, it might be interesting to you if you're UPS because it means that your prospect might be at the FedEx headquarters. If you are selling luxury jets and your prospect's list of people she follows consists of mostly retail store employees, you might have to determine whether she has the funds to actually pay for the aircraft. If you see that your prospect is on vacation (or maybe your competitor), you'll know what actions might come from that. People volunteer lots of information via their social networking presence every single day.

- If you consider your sales activities-based, such as helping people reduce their concerns with their purchase decision, you can use your Google+ page to educate. Post YouTube videos demonstrating how simple your product or service is to use, post testimonials from satisfied customers, or post interviews with people who make up the community you serve.

- Another way you can improve your sales success is by offering video hangouts where you educate the buyers about the product they own. By nurturing your existing buyers and by helping them to use what you sell for their own success, you'll improve potential word of mouth. If you get them using the product or service more, there's a better potential for renewal. See?

- The least useful way to use Google+ for sales is by trying to sell directly via the platform. Unless you're selling something that might appeal to the early adopter set or a somewhat more tech-friendly set, it's a lot harder to convert someone to a purchase directly from your Google+ account. Instead, think of ways you can use Google+ to keep the sales cycle warm. That's what will get you to the finish line.

How to Set Up Your Local Business on Google+

Because Google shifted Google Places away and into Google+ Local, at least 80 million business pages already exist in this new format. It's an exciting addition to what a business owner can do with Google+. Let's talk about what it takes to implement Google+ for your local business with these first steps:

1. Currently, to start an account on Google+ Local (which replaces Google Places), you don't go to http://www.google.com/local. You go to http://google.com/places. To claim your business, click the Get Started Now button. On the page that displays, verify that you're the owner of the business.

2. Next, a page displays where you can verify the address of your location or locations, you can write a useful About section, you can add your hours of operations, you can add photos, and so on. Hint: The more you do here, the more it'll look like you're a business and not a ghost town.

 Note

Most Google+ Local pages are ghost towns because most businesses don't know they have happened.

There are also reviews available for most (if not all) businesses registered in this way. I'm not concerned with how to remove a bad review. (There are ways to request this.) Instead, one point I want to make is that a review—even a negative one—is an opportunity to interact with people about the service they experience from your business.

Should you choose to respond to a review, remember these guidelines:

- Don't be defensive. People consider a harsh pushback to be distasteful.

- But don't be a pushover. If someone is clearly in the wrong, you're welcome to write a brief (brief!) rebuttal explaining your position.

- The best reviews are those that point out that your business isn't for them, especially if you don't want others seeking the same experience. If you sell vacuum cleaners and someone comes in looking for opera lessons, a great review says, "I can't believe that this place doesn't offer opera lessons." Get me?

- The best way to handle review complaints is offline. Mention in your reply that you'll contact the person, and then do so offline. A back and forth on your Local page isn't useful.

- Remember that your Local page isn't exactly your business page. If you want to list specials and the like, that can happen on your Google+ business page. This Local page needs to be filled out, it needs to be policed, and it needs to be cared for on a quarterly basis, but that's not where you'll spend most of your time.

How to Use a Google+ Business Page to Your Best Advantage

When I wrote the first edition of the book, business pages had been released for approximately an hour or so. Now, several months later, a lot of the previous annoyances have gone away (told you so), and yet, many companies are still not getting a lot of push out of what they're trying to accomplish there. With that said, here's a quick recipe card for people who want to use Google+ to maintain an outpost for a brand or business page, specifically.

- The basics apply. Be sure to make an amazing About page and to include all kinds of useful information. Please put one or two human names people can contact. It's hard to contact Intel. It's much easier to reach out to Becky Brown (director of social media at Intel).

- The photos section becomes useful insofar as it can offer some interesting pictures of your products, your services, your happy customers, your employees, and other interesting happenings. When I went to Intel's business page, there's a picture of a U.S. presidential visit to the campus. Though I'm not one for bragging, that certainly caught my attention.

- In posting, I've noticed that the difference between the "big guys" and the "very small businesses" is that the big guys come off more like personable people who want to share interesting content and the little guys look like they're desperate to get a sale. Hint: You want to seem less desperate.

Consider posting information that's useful to the person who uses your product or service. For instance, at the Williams-Sonoma page (https://plus.google.com/+Williams-Sonoma/), I saw a post about a chef from a Brooklyn area restaurant, who shares a recipe for halibut and shellfish. They post a gorgeous photo and then a link to the standalone blog for this project (souschefseries.com). The post is rich with pictures, helpful ideas, and various links to even more helpful information, and at the bottom, after all this value from the company, there are three big pictures of three products that are used in preparing a dish like this.

It's one of the best methods for selling, at least according to my friend Anthony Iannarino of TheSalesBlog.com: give value, give more value, and then offer to be helpful in providing the product or service you're selling.

- Share a bit of you. Rebecca Dillon of Rebecca's Soap Delicatessen has a mix of posts selling her own products plus posts serving the space she covers (a link to a free ebook on beauty, for instance). And then what I found wonderful was that she shared a post about her choice of television viewing. Think about how soap is sold. There's not a lot to say: it's got this in it or it doesn't have that in it. It smells nice. It lathers. Whatever. Rebecca has added a potential interaction by posting this, and I've seen people rush in to comment on her post.

You don't necessarily have to share what you're going to watch on Hulu Plus to accomplish this, but whatever you choose to share, make it something that isn't related to your product or service, but that isn't so far afield that people still want to interact with you. The goal is to share a bit of who you are, so that people may or may not buy from you based on your personality and/or the personality (personalities) that make up your company.

The rapper and actor Curtis Jackson (50 Cent) shares plenty about his upcoming projects (https://plus.google.com/+50Cent/) and the occasional behind-the-scenes moment. On the day I wrote this, he was also mourning the loss of a friend, which humanizes him to people who want to see beyond his persona.

Share what makes sense. In the realm of sentences I never thought I'd type, this one is fairly close to the top: "Check out how Britney Spears shares what she does on her page (https://plus.google.com/+britneyspears/)." That said, notice that she (or whoever maintains her page because I don't know whether she does or not) includes a bunch of self-promotion, but she's also sharing a lot of material that she finds interesting, such as a music video that's making the rounds, behind-the-scenes material, and other nuggets of interest.

I won't go deep into what it takes to make a celebrity page work, because most of us reading this book aren't in that category, but what we can learn from celebrities is that they spend a lot of time trying to build emotional bridges between their fan base and their persona. You can use this mindset to help you with your own recipe for success.

The Personal Versus Business Page Recipe

This section cheats with the format for creating a recipe, but be patient. I am asked often whether someone should spend more time on making business relationships via their personal page or via their business page. In recipe form, here's the answer as it stands today. This is subject to change as business pages evolve.

- Your personal page lets you connect with people whether or not they've chosen to circle you (see my point about the vampire problem in Chapter 1, "How Did I Get Here?"). This means that your personal page is a lot more powerful.

- If you've got a business page but your business is populated by only a handful of people (say, under 100 employees), then it's a bit unnecessary, as the voice of the brand is you. It might be okay to keep a brand page for later use, but if so, use this brand page to highlight your personal page(s) and make sure people know that's how you interact with them. A "ghost town" branding page is a bad sign, no matter what.

  If you have a business with many employees and more than one voice of the brand, you'll want to promote your branded page, but also to let employees maintain their own presence. Dell does this. They have over 6,300 trained social media professionals and they maintain only one brand page (at the time of this writing). The people who make Dell what it is are given the microphone, so to speak. Instead of looking only at the branded page, you can talk with Michael Dell, Richard Binhammer, Lionel Menchaca, Susan Beebe, and many more. That's a nice way to go, I think, if you're a larger company.

- We have this strange "worry" problem when it comes to acquiring Internet accounts. All the good URLs are taken. To that end, I see a lot of "squatting" already on various Google+ brand pages and plenty of "words that might make good brand pages later." I can't predict the future, but I can say that it's a lot more effort to worry about such things than it is to worry about doing business, making sales, keeping your customers happy, and so on. That's an opinion. You can do with it as you wish.

Are There More Recipes You Want?

Of course there are more recipes, as I don't cover how to do this or what to do when that happens. If you want, send me an email at chris@chrisbrogan.com. I'll answer your questions, even if it takes a couple of days. In the mean time, please realize that there's a lot to cover and a lot to get done and although it appears as if everything is not in place, and even if you're worried that people aren't there, most of what I've covered in this chapter of recipes is useful to you even if people aren't crawling all over your posts just yet. This is what it takes to get ready to go for business. Get to it and see what comes of your efforts. I promise that you'll definitely not do any worse implementing this advice.

18

Next Steps

We've covered a lot in this book. I've tried not to talk too specifically about the features and technology aspects of Google+ because the tools are still evolving and because they aren't the most interesting part of using the platform. What scares most people about a new social network such as Google+ is learning how to click everything that needs to be clicked and how to avoid doing something embarrassing. Though those are important parts of the learning process, what we have talked about in this book focuses more on the business opportunities inherent in using Google+ as part of your outpost strategy for your digital channel.

This chapter sums up some potential next steps, in case you've mostly been reading along and haven't jumped into action. Now that we've talked at length about various aspects of Google+, from those "day-in-the-life" glimpses to understanding how to execute a "warm sell," to thoughts on how to circle people and develop a content strategy, let's outline some of that here. I don't want to repeat what we've already covered, but it's important to give it order and also provide a simple reference section.

Starting Moves

Following is a list of initial steps you can take:

- Decide who in the organization should be involved in Google+ for business. The more the merrier, but this depends on your business and on how you intend to implement it.

- Determine whether you'll use standard Gmail accounts or if you'll use Google Applications accounts. (There's technically no difference, but for a level of enhanced business branding, if you use your Google Apps accounts, you can use corporate or alternative-to-corporate business email addresses.)

- Write a simple "rules of engagement" document (no more than one page in length) that spells out the simplest possible goals of anyone's interactions on Google+, which spells out the absolute no-no's and off-limits behaviors (such as trashing competitors) and explains what to do if something goes wrong.

- Consider a "launch day" (or days) to gather people together and train them about the uses of Google+ and so that you can reiterate the policy you've put together for the rules of engagement. Remember that different departments (if you're a larger company) will have different goals, and that this might actually be the point where it becomes clear that people see the possibilities of using Google+ differently. Also remember that some people won't feel as technically comfortable, so this is your chance to help them feel a bit more acclimated.

- It would be exceptionally good to invite the Legal department (if you're a larger company or if you're highly regulated) to this experience far earlier.

- For everyone you decide should have access to Google+ in the company, build robust profiles. You might put some guidelines in place for what should go into a profile, but I'd also encourage some flexibility in this area after covering specific corporate goals. For instance, don't enforce corporate ID photos as the standard avatar photos for Google+. Be creative and permissive, but with some "bumpers" in place so that people know what won't be okay in the profile-creating process.

- Put together a "cheat sheet" of how to delete a post, how to share a post, how to set circles specifically for sharing, and any other matters that might prove immediately useful to employees who find themselves in a bind.

Listening

Listening on the social web is a matter of implementing search tools to understand what people are saying about you, your brand, your competitors, and more. This is really the secret gold of using social tools for business.

- Google+ enables you to cook up repeat searches. Simply put your search terms up in the bar at the top of the page, and then select Save Search to keep a copy of that search on your left sidebar.

- Build searches for your products, your services, your company name, any location that's specific to your business, and maybe even your competitors' information, and use these frequently to see who's talking about you.

- Be diligent to the Notifications part of Google+, but realize that it won't catch every mention of you or your business. Use both the search feature plus the notifications system to find people who could use help.

- If you have one department listening on behalf of the whole company, have a simple routing policy that tells this person how to send post information to the appropriate party. For instance, if your PR department manages your Google+ presence, but it sees a customer service request, it would want to forward this to the appropriate customer service person, and if that PR person finds a sales lead, he should know how to move that lead along to the appropriate salesperson.

- Realize that there are many ways to search for opportunities. For instance, I posted back in November 2011, about point-and-shoot cameras, asking what everyone was using. If you represented Panasonic or Sony or any of those companies, wouldn't you want a moment to tell me about your latest and greatest? There's revenue to be had in searching based on whatever one might be saying that invokes an interest in your product or service. Test this quite frequently and tweak your search terms as you learn what brings you more opportunity.

Posting

Consider an editorial calendar, where you encourage team contributions to posting. If you think about it, this is another point where you might discover cross-purposes in the use of Google+. In a larger company, imagine the kind of post and frequency of posts a salesperson might want to see. What about the marketing department and the PR department? What do they need? How can the senior team engage? Does support run your social media? Whatever the mix, if you push together one or two teams or disciplines into one Google+ business page, for instance, you need to put together an editorial calendar that explains which posts are coming out when so that you have a balanced approach.

If you encourage employees to post on their own pages, be flexible enough to allow (maybe even encourage) personal posts. Realize that we are all humans seeking to interact with other humans. If you sent your sales team to a conference to find prospects, you wouldn't expect them to lead with talk about your world-changing products. You'd encourage them to make small talk and find points of similarity between themselves and their prospects. The same is true of Google+. By learning about the person behind the employee, many a better business relationship can be forged.

If you decide to adopt some kind of "vetting" process for posts, realize that the more complicated or red-tape filled this is, the less interest employees will have in posting. I've seen many corporations do a great job of getting their legal team involved early in the process to build out communications plans, and this tends to work best. Unless you're in a highly regulated industry, put up the simplest of bumpers to help your employees know where the boundaries are, and then let them experiment a bit.

Encourage sharing, as well, so that employees don't simply post the company news and the company's perspective. The more your prospects and customers feel that you're sharing information that's useful to them, not just information that helps sell your product, the more trust those prospects and customers will have, and the more your efforts can take on a community feeling versus a sales feeling.

As stated elsewhere, posts with pictures get more engagement than posts without pictures. Slightly longer posts (more than 100 words) but not vast posts (more than 1,000) words will get more comments than those outside those margins. Video posts often get fewer comments, but that doesn't mean people didn't find the videos interesting. (The experience of video tends to make us lean back and not type as much.)

Posting frequency is something of an art more than a science. For instance, if your posts matter only to a certain geography, you don't have to worry about finding the sweet spot in four or more time zones. If you're a media brand such as *Wired Magazine*, you will likely post more often in a day than if you are Glynne's Soaps. As a starting point, consider putting up four posts a day, either every 6 hours (if you serve the world at large) or across the morning, early afternoon, late afternoon, and evening (if you're central to a single time zone). Post repetition is not a crime, but it might bug some of your followers. On Twitter, it's great to repeat posts because they flow through the stream quickly and get lost. That's not as much the case on Google+, so I don't recommend a lot of post repetition. For instance, if you're having a contest and there's a time deadline, it probably won't be a great idea to promote that contest every few hours every day. Try mixing those promotions in with other content.

Sharing

Following are some pointers for sharing:

- Sharing is caring. Make sure to cover sharing in all your strategy and policy conversations.

- Cross-sharing only your employees' posts and other related brands will come off as cheesy. Use this as a condiment and not an entree.

- The "killer" move in sharing is to sometimes point out something interesting your competitor is doing. If Ford Motor Company can do it in the highly competitive world of automobile sales, you can consider doing it in your own business.

- Sharing your customers' and prospects' posts is a great way to encourage interaction because it shows that you care about what they're talking about just as much as you care about helping them with your own products and services.

- On Twitter, I've often said that a 12:1 them-to-you ratio of sharing is good, where you talk about other people 12 times as often as you talk about your own products and services. This wouldn't work as well on Google+, so think about it as more of a 1:4 them-to-you, such that you post or share something about someone else 1 time for every 4 times you talk about yourself. The difference is that conversations can happen under the posts and that lets you have the interaction that is important in a way that's more robust and deeper than Twitter.

Video

Following are some pointers for posting video:

- If you've not yet built a company YouTube channel, head over to YouTube.com and set one up.

- Your commercials are probably the least interesting thing you can share on Google+, unless they are hilarious and award-winning. Otherwise, skip them.

- Testimonials make for great content, especially if you focus more on making the buyer the hero and less on talking about how amazing your own products are. Keep testimonials under 3 minutes, and ask for specifics on how your customers achieved success (without pushing them too hard to talk about your products and services).

- Product demos are a great way to use video for your business needs. Again, try to keep these brief. People's attention span on video is measured at less than 2 minutes. You can do longer form work, but mix that in with other shorter video posts.

- If you're a professional speaker, you can do video samples of your speeches. Presenters can do a video capture of their slide deck. Authors can read parts of their books on video. The opportunities for this are endless.

- Interviews are a great way to use video. I'm a Mac user and I use Call Recorder for Skype to shoot simple two person videos. You can also use more professional tools such as GoToMeeting with HDFaces.

- I've also used another Mac tool, Screenflow, to capture a Google Hangout with great success. Thus, if you want to capture a user group meeting or a product demo in hangouts, you can do that. Remember to be explicit that you intend to record the session, and so on. You might not need to go so far as to secure release paperwork, but that depends how you intend to use the video.

- A "behind the scenes" at your company can be fun, too. People love to see what's not normally seen. Take them on a walk through your restaurant. Invite them to part of the company barbecue (especially if you're hiring). Give your audience a glimpse into a different side of your business. It works wonders on relationship-building.

- Remember that Google (the search engine) can't see what goes on inside a video. Consider putting some highlights (for keyword value) in the text of your video post above the video. This also encourages people to click and watch because they'll better understand what they're getting themselves into.

- You can always add links to the post where you share the video so that if you want to point people to the product page or your service offering or your book (or whatever you're selling), you can do so. I did a video walkthrough of the various tools I use to create video, and I provided Amazon affiliate links and made quite a bit of money selling the products I mentioned in my walkthrough.

- Don't forget that you can share and curate other people's videos. If you're lucky enough to have a product or service that other people have recorded videos about, and you like the videos, share them. I watched a great user-generated video by an Audi driver who wanted to take his Audi R8 into the snow to see how it would fare. The company later put part of that user's video into an official TV commercial, but if I were an Audi dealer, I'd most definitely show that video (the original, not the commercial) as proof of why the car is a great buy.

- Some of your employees (maybe even the senior team) will do much better recording short video updates than they will with writing posts. Go with it. It's personable and gives the company a much more human face.

Hangouts

There's no feature inside of Google+ that is more suited for being the secret sauce of your business. From internal to external uses, the Hangout is a winner. Following are a few thoughts on getting started with Hangouts:

- Of course, you can always have a hangout just to have it. This is the easiest kind, where you turn on the camera and invite the public or your prospects or your internal colleagues to just have a conversation. But that's just the tip of the iceberg.

- Customer service can offer "office hours" for your customers, such that people can get video-supported help. This is especially useful if the product is something in which visual can help. Screen sharing also can take place, which is helpful.

- You can offer classes and tutorials. Think about how much more fun it would be to use your new yo-yo, if you got lessons from a yo-yo master. (Do you sell yo-yos?)

- Michael Dell, CEO of Dell, uses hangouts to talk about interesting news related to his company and the industry at large. It's a cool opportunity, if you've got the company or team that people want to know about. If you're the best roofer in Schenectady, that might not be a great way to use a hangout.

- My favorite possible use is to connect an expert in the field you service to the people who might normally use your product. For instance, if you sell running shoes, how cool would it be to have Dean Karnazes on to talk about what it takes to run ultramarathons? If you are a publisher, why not have a quick writing lesson from Chuck Palahniuk?

- With hangouts, remember that moderation is a tricky beast. I've already been in a few hangouts where people have come in and caused a bit of a ruckus, so be aware that it could happen to you. I imagine Google+ will implement better moderation tools in the future.

- Hangouts in the time of important news would be interesting, too. You can have "roving reporters" at your company events. You might even set up your event to answer a few questions from the hangout.

- Walkthroughs can be fun if you do a mobile hangout or if you use a laptop and Wi-Fi. Imagine taking someone on a tour of your restaurant in real time. It's not the kind of thing that fits neatly into a repeatable strategy, but it most definitely would leave a lasting impression from time to time.

- Finally, and somewhat related to my "pairing experts with your community" opportunity, it could be fun to pay for some sponsored conversations. For instance, as mentioned in the business pages chapter, if *Forbes* invited in Warren Buffett for a talk, and people could join the hangout, that would make for some compelling content (and potentially a premium revenue stream for *Forbes*).

Photos

Sharing photos on Google+ is a powerful tool. Many experiences start around a simple photo share. Following are some tips for photo sharing:

- If you have products, by all means, post a few photos into Google+. People will find them interesting. If there are concept sketches, share those, too. Everyone loves the back story.

- One interesting point about sharing photos when considering your business objectives is that pictures with people can warm up your story.

Put a photo of a happy buyer (not stock photography) on your page and share a testimonial. It will get more engagement every time.

- Put a photo with any post of text that you do, no matter what. People engage more with posts that contain a photo. Don't believe this? It's simple to test. Post something with a photo and post something without to see how many comments, pluses, and shares you get on each. It will almost invariably be the piece with a photo that gets shared and interacted with more.

Commenting

Commenting is an important (and often overlooked) part of using any social network, including Google+. If you're not commenting, you're missing the chance to take an interaction beyond the eye-batting and into the "get ready for a kiss" stage (to paraphrase Carrie Wilkerson). Following are some tips for commenting:

- Be the #1 contributor to the comments on your pages (your user account and/or your business page). If someone spends time talking with you, do your best to comment back. Don't methodically answer every comment that comes in, but try to add something when people comment. It makes them feel seen and heard. (True story: As I wrote this part of the post, I realized that I hadn't walked this talk today, so I stopped writing this part of the book, ran back to my Google+ account, and started commenting back on what people had shared with me.)

- One of the best ways to find more people who want to circle you is to comment in meaningful (and never spammy) ways on other people's posts. If you find posts that would be of interest to your community, share something useful that isn't self-promoting, and you'll likely pick up new followers who will add you to their circle. Commenting is usually where I find new people to circle these days.

- Comments are a great way to add more flavor to an initial post. Start by posting, then see what people say initially, and flavor the rest of the conversation by adding comments and supporting material.

- Remember that this is the same as in sales conversations, education on a product, or anything else you might do in person or over the phone. Just also remember that this is "in public" and if you're working to resolve a customer service issue, it might be best to take it offline, so you can interact better and resolve the problem together.

- Negative comments are a *blessing*. Spam is one thing. Push the spam button. But do *not* delete negative comments, if they are reasonable.

Censorship based on sentiment is never a good policy. Swearing, sure, delete those. Is a comment not related to the conversation and content? Fine, delete it. But do *not* delete comments simply because they are negative or critical of your company. Respond. Do your best to turn the situation around. Never fight, but also don't kowtow. A whole book could be written around what to do and what not to do with the opportunity gifted to you by a negative comment.

Business Pages

Following are some guidelines for creating your business pages:

- "Live" in your page and post there before you start promoting it. People who come to a business page with one or two posts and barely any information on the about page won't likely be sticking around. Treat the page with some care and feeding before you try to grow a community around it.

- Seek community members by commenting intelligently with your individual account on various posts, and by creating interesting information on your personal posts, with a link to your new business page.

- Realize that a Google+ business page is a great "outpost" to connect with people where they're already using social networks, and that it is best used as an adjunct to your primary web presence, your "home base." This strategy hasn't changed much in a few years and doesn't change with Google+.

- Think of your business page as a TV station, a magazine, and a fancy business card. The goal isn't to get people to fall in love with your business page. The goal is to do business.

- In creating interesting posts via your business page, realize that most people want to get a sense of belonging. Talking about yourself (your company) on your business page all the time is like going to a cocktail party and when you meet people, talking all about your stuff without asking them about themselves.

Some Final Thoughts

If you've made it this far, you clearly have an interest in using this great new social medium. I've been fortunate enough to talk with many of the early adopters of this platform who work in various levels of business, and I have also spoken with some of the people who cover the emerging technology industry, such as Guy Kawasaki, former Apple evangelist for the Macintosh and serial entrepreneur and bestselling author. We concur that Google+ has a big shot at being a long-lasting and successful platform for doing business.

If I can leave you with one lasting piece of advice that transcends the actual technology of Google+, it's this: People do business with people they like. This is one of those simple sentences that people nod about, and then they go back to interacting in ways that don't encourage a lot of "like-ability." When faced with marketers and business owners asking me about these technologies and how they drive business growth, I'm always asked for the "fastest," the "cheapest," and the "easiest" way to "use" social media to grow business.

Fast. Cheap. Easy. This works great with hamburgers. It doesn't usually work well with relationships that you hope to have lasting value. The truth is, social media business tools don't scale well. Nothing I've explained in this book is as "easy" as putting out a huge advertising campaign that blankets billboards, buses, radios, and televisions. Nothing here is as "fast" as giving your customers a phone tree to navigate instead of a warm human voice. Nothing I espouse in these practices is as "easy" as beating your email list until your buyer buys something (once).

Loyalty isn't fast, cheap, or easy. Valuable customers/clients aren't fast, cheap, or easy. Success doesn't come fast, cheap, or easy. Starting from the position of, "How can I do this in the least amount of time, with the least effort, and get the most return on my effort?" is the worst way to think about your use of social networks and social media. First, it doesn't sound like you're putting any effort into that. Do you know what they call a fat person who has a gym membership? A fat person who has a gym membership. Know what they call that same person should they choose to *use* the gym membership over months and years? Successful and fit.

Also think about this: Never invest solely in the platform. Invest in your buyer. Go where they are. If Google+ comes and goes, as all things do, you'll want to have used your time wisely on the platform, by building relationships with your buyers and your prospects. Spend money on people, not the platform. Spend money on being able to afford the time to build relationships of value for your company. The benefits over time (want a great metric: lifelong dollar value of your happy customers) is the endgame.

A Note About This Book

Because this technology is a moving target, I'll be keeping a running log of updates to the book at my personal blog, http://chrisbrogan.com, thanks to the people at Que publishing. If you want to follow along and stay updated with any changes and additions to the original book (in between editions), bookmark the following secret-to-you URL:

http://chrisbrogan.com/gplusb12

This page is password protected, and your password is

friend

(Nerds who have read a certain series of books featuring a wizard long before anyone had ever heard of Hogwarts might appreciate the reference.)

You and I will stay in touch about the updates there. Work for you?

And if you want to connect with me on Google+, I'd love to hear from you. Reach me by going to http://chrisbrogan.com/plus.

A

Interesting People to Circle on Google+

The people listed in this appendix are in no particular order. Each of these people is interesting and worth consideration as a kind of "starter pack" of people to follow and interact with on Google+.

Robert Scoble (https://plus.google.com/+Scobleizer/posts): Robert talks about tech, startups, the future, and more. He is quite prolific, so you'll likely want to put him in a circle with others who fit that category. That said, I find his posts interesting and I like him as a person.

Sean Bonner (https://plus.google.com/101629211371073711149/posts): I don't know Sean's real title, but when I want to be entertained, I follow what Sean has to say.

Lynette Young (https://plus.google.com/+LynetteYoung/posts): Among other reasons to follow her, Lynette runs Women of Google+, a list of interesting women who use the service. She's also the author of a book by Que, *Google+ for Small Businesses*, so she has a lot to offer.

Guy Kawasaki (https://plus.google.com/+GuyKawasaki/posts): Guy's another person for your "posts often" circle. He has a lot of ideas and shares interesting information. He's definitely worth paying attention to if you want to get quite a potpourri of thoughts across your box.

Scott Beale, Laughing Squid (https://plus.google.com/+LaughingSquid): Scott Beale runs the Laughing Squid, which has a variety of posts about pop culture and fun parts of the Internet. On any given day, you'll find YouTube videos of cats attacking a mail slot, pictures of weird hot dogs, and much more.

Mike Elgan (https://plus.google.com/+MikeElgan/): Mike is a media maker, reporter, and storyteller. He also does a great job of finding interesting up-and-comers and pointing them out to others, so you'll not just learn what Mike has to share, but you'll find some amazing people to circle by getting to know him.

Steven Hodson (https://plus.google.com/+StevenHodson/): I've been a fan of Steven's work for years. On Google+, he shares a blend of interesting information. Note that I've mentioned many people in this appendix who are more about sharing and finding interesting information that hails from elsewhere. It is all about what one shares.

Craig Newmark (https://plus.google.com/+CraigNewmark/): Sure, he founded Craigslist, but that's not why to follow Craig. He's got his eyes on several important issues, such as the future of government, veteran's causes, and even birds. We've only sat down for coffee once, but through his Google+ posts, I feel connected to Craig every day.

Shira Lazar (https://plus.google.com/+ShiraLazar/): Media maker and trend finder, Lazar is the host of the popular web television show *What's Trending*. She finds great stuff from the realm of pop culture and gives plenty of interesting angles to her posts.

Esther Schindler (https://plus.google.com/106875990476951662693): An editor and writer and someone who seems to know everyone, Esther creates and/or finds interesting material to contemplate. If you're not into tech, you're not as likely to enjoy Esther, but if you are, she has interesting material.

Additional Plus Starter Packs

Just to be clear, these are some people to consider following. I selected them out of people I follow and who I think are interesting. This isn't a directory. It's just a list of names to get you started or to give you ideas. Discover who comments on their posts and follows them, and grow your list from those names if you choose.

Artists

Todd Jordan (https://plus.google.com/103929313090037971278)

Rodney Pike (https://plus.google.com/s/rodney%20pike)

Brands

Ford Motor Company (https://plus.google.com/+ford/)

Pepsi (https://plus.google.com/111883881632877146615)

B&H (https://plus.google.com/+BandH/)

Businesses

Sir Richard Branson (https://plus.google.com/+RichardBranson/)

John Jantsch (https://plus.google.com/+JohnJantsch/)

Carrie Wilkerson (https://plus.google.com/104846472501579099769)

Charles H. Green (https://plus.google.com/112406923989516013432/)

Celebs

Jeri Ryan (https://plus.google.com/+JeriRyan)

Wil Wheaton (https://plus.google.com/+WilWheaton/)

50 Cent (https://plus.google.com/+50Cent/)

Photographers

Trey Ratcliff (https://plus.google.com/+TreyRatcliff/)

Thomas Hawk (https://plus.google.com/+ThomasHawk)

Other Sites and Resources to Check Out

Find People on Plus (http://findpeopleonplus.com)

Mashable's Google+ Guide (http://mashable.com/2011/07/16/google-plus-guide/)

Women of Google+ (http://womenofgplus.com)

Index

Q–R

S

W

X–Y–Z